EVA R. PRIESTLEY

A GIRL NAMED EVA

- A MEMOIR -

FOREWORD

If only I had paid more attention, asked questions, and written everything down when my mother talked about her early life! I had the perfect chance, for, as she got older, she came to live with my family. Her stories were of innocent childhood pranks, of joys, fears, and disappointments. She spoke of World War I, which broke out when she was seven years old, and of the struggle for survival after that war and during the Great Depression. Yes, I blew my chance. It is too late now, and I have to live with my regrets.

During the precious few years of having my father around, before the war, which, in Germany, began in 1939, we did barely any reminiscing. How often, after all, do young children ask, "Daddy, what was it like when you were a little boy?" And so, unfortunately, I only know a few sketchy facts about my father's early days. Most of those tidbits have been handed down to me by my mother and by my aunt, Tante Dora, his younger sister.

Though I have spent many years with my maternal grandmother, not many stories of her youth have reached my ears, and I know even less about my grandfather, her husband, for he was a man of few words.

If anyone would pry for facts about my paternal grandparents, their backgrounds, their siblings, or how they have spent their young days, I could only answer with a shrug and a blank stare.

I do not wish this ignorance about me to happen to my descendants. Eventually, during some quiet moments, perhaps while leafing through my many photo albums, or at a family gathering, they may begin to wonder about the olden days and how Mom, Grandma, Great-grandma, or whatever they call me, has lived through them.

Originally, the story of my early life was only intended for my own family. But then something unexpected happened. As I read the manuscript, in small installments, to my students and my friends, they clamored to hear more. European-born friends compared their experiences with mine. My American listeners, eager to learn about "the other side," urged me to make my story public.

So ... open my book of memoirs and begin to read, and you'll soon find out how I have spent my early childhood and the not-so-calm days of my youth in Germany, my native country.

Before you get started, I want you to know that only the recollections of Eva, the girl, are being offered here. Whoever wants to learn more about the political events of the years I have covered has to do his research somewhere else.

CHAPTER ONE

A STROKE OF FATE

Nineteen forty-five has begun. News from the East and the West are discouraging. German troops are pulling back. Everything so easily conquered at the beginning of the war will soon be completely gone. In one of his last letters, Papa advises my mother to guard Gisela and me well. He writes something like, "When the Russian soldiers come, be as cunning as a fox, as vicious as a snake, and as protective as a mother bear of her cubs." Mama seems jittery after that. She must be very much afraid of what is in store for us.

Toward the end of January, chaos begins. For weeks, streams of refugees, ferried from farther east of Pomerania, pass through Neuendorf, our small village on the Baltic island of Wollin. We shudder at the sight of all those homeless people. People on horse-drawn wagons, people pulling carts, people pushing wheelbarrows laden with meager, earthly possessions – or with something more precious like a sick child, a disabled spouse, or a grandparent too weak to walk. Some simply carry a few belongings on their backs or in their arms. All try to escape the atrocities committed by the bent-on-revenge soldiers of the conquering Russian army.

I see misery, hopelessness, dejection, and it breaks my young heart.

5

When the main road ceases to be clogged with human wretchedness on wheels and on foot, and the dead, left along the way, are buried, the retreating German foot soldiers come through. They are a tired, miserable-looking lot, just like the refugees.

My mother goes to the road and asks as many of the men as she possibly can, "Have you seen my brother, Willi Krause?"

"No."

"Is Willi Krause among you?"

They shake their heads.

"My brother, Willi Krause, is missing. Has anyone heard of him?"

"No. We're so sorry."

Then, one day, two army trucks arrive and park in front of the by now defunct post office. The drivers offer a free ride to anyone who wants to flee the island.

"Let's go back home to Berlin," says Mama.

In a great hurry, she gathers some clothes, food, documents, and whatever else seems of absolute importance, and then she informs Frau Teetzen, our landlady, of her decision to leave.

"Please, don't go," begs the woman. "Stay."

"I'm sorry, but it's best we leave now. We thank you so much for your kindness. Take care. *Auf Wiedersehen.*"

Marie Teetzen has tears in her eyes as she bids us farewell.

Soon we are sitting in the bed of one of the big trucks. Mama is in the middle; Gisela, my younger sister, and I are on either side of her. Our bags and bundles serve as seats.

Gisela is frightened, I know. I am mainly stunned by the unexpected turn of events.

The vehicle slowly fills with nervous people, mostly evacuees like us, all trying to reach their respective cities or relatives and friends further west.

A handful of "natives" joins us, probably those afraid of the consequences of their political affiliations and activities. They are the minor party members who probably don't have to quiver for their lives. The bigwigs have already departed before them – in secret.

Suddenly, Mama gets edgy. Then she tenses. She appears to be listening to something. She turns around … and listens some more. Then she yanks us by our arms.

"Gather your things and get off the truck," she orders. "We're not going."

"But why?" Gisela asks in her small, scared voice.

"I heard something. It was like a command. We should obey the voice that came to me."

As we jump off the truck, pulling our belongings behind us, other people follow. They have heard Mama's words, and they take them as a message meant for them, too.

When we reappear at the house on Wiesenstraße, Frau Teetzen can hardly contain her joy.

Sad news reaches our village the next day. The ferry, going from the island to the mainland, has been bombarded and sunk. All passengers have been killed. We are not among the dead.

"I told you I have a sixth sense," says my mother.

I believe it has been a case of divine intervention. And without this miracle in the early part of 1945, I would never have been able to tell my story.

CHAPTER TWO

THE CALM

I try to look back into my early childhood, as far as I possibly can. It's hard.

Medical scientists say the unborn can already hear from inside the womb, and the learning process begins before birth. Therefore, I gather, the brain should have in storage what the tiny ear of the fetus has perceived.

Oh, I don't really want to delve into the time before I breathed air, but it would be nice to know about my very first impressions on that very important day, April 5, 1932, when I was born.

What was it like when I laid eyes on my mother's smiling face? I assume she was happy to see me and satisfied that I had all my fingers and toes and no birthmarks or other deformities, unless a bit too long and skinny made me look less beautiful than the tiny angel she'd probably expected. Did I enjoy her gentle touch? Did I like her soft voice, now heard clearly and not muffled by the various walls that had encased me inside her tummy?

What did I think of the babble all around me? And how was it when I discovered my own voice? Was it hard to practice those first sounds? At what point did I realize that it would be nice to move around like the big people? Did my efforts to imitate them frustrate me?

9

I was told I took my first steps in the crib, holding on to my little blanket, when I was just six months old. Did I realize what feat that was? Perhaps I considered it nothing more spectacular than standing by the rails of my bed, doing knee flexes and tiny hops for hours on end. My mother may have exaggerated the length of time, but I wouldn't know. I was merely a baby, and my memory of it went poof!

I also cannot recall that I was a terrible screamer - supposedly - whenever I saw my mother go out the door. She only went to the mailbox, or to bring in wood or coal from the shed, or water from the outside pump. How was I to know? She could've been leaving for good, making me a motherless child. But I only learned about my annoying vocal performance and the crib exercises from my mother, who probably wanted to let me know that I had not been a perfect youngster.

When I finally manage to penetrate the thick fog that shrouds my very young years and discover something, it's like looking through a tiny peephole. Just an itsy- bitsy glimpse I get, and not even quite clear, of a tiny child - me!

I can see myself as a toddler, not much more than eighteen months old. That's a rough calculation, taking into account the time of my mother's difficult pregnancy, when she was carrying my sister. For a long time, she couldn't keep food down, and she almost died.

Anyhow, there I am, climbing from a little stool onto the kitchen chair, and then onto the bench to the left, by the wall, that holds two water buckets. The space not taken up by the bucket closest to me is not large, and I have to be extremely careful where I put my foot. I have to find the right spot so I won't fall. And, somehow, I have to steady myself with my left hand. Do I hold on to the full bucket? I can't remember. In my right hand I have a cup. I dip it into the bucket and fill it with water. Careful, careful! I must not spill it. And I must not fall. But I'm like a little monkey and manage all right. If some drops of water hit the chair or the floor - or both - I cannot see through my little window into the past. All that matters is that the water gets to my poor, dear mother, who is on her bed, so very, very sick and in need of a drink.

I have a vague recollection of my grandmother, Oma, being in the house for a while, taking care of me. That bit of memory stems either from the time of my mother's hospitalization to save her life during that pregnancy or from when my sister, Gisela, was born on March 30, 1934.

It puzzles me greatly that no picture of my newborn sibling can be brought into focus. I'm certain that I was pleased to have the baby in the house, especially, since she was a pleasant addition to the family, one who didn't scream as much and as loud as I had done - according to my mother, and I believe it. Gisela, in later years, was always the quieter, shyer one.

For some strange reason, an image of my father doesn't come up until the summer of 1934, several

months after my second birthday. He carries me.
I'm not satisfied being in his arms. I want my
mother. But she's holding Gisela, the sleeping baby.
I kick and scream. The passengers in the crowded
trolley - we're on our way home from visiting my
grandparents in the city - give me ugly looks. My
father attempts to pacify me, and his grip tightens.
My mother tries to reason with me for a while, but
when my screams hit a crescendo, she resorts to
scolding. It must've been a great relief for my
parents to come to the stop where we had to get off,
and to escape the disapproving glances and the head
shaking of the other trolley riders.

What happens next? Do I receive the deserved
whack on the behind? Who knows! Perhaps, all
worn out from the fuss, I put my head on my father's
shoulder and fall asleep. I'm probably overtired,
anyhow.

The whack, by the way, would've been meted out
by my mother. She is the one who, off and on, uses
her hand to give us kids a smack, but never a real
hard one. My father is always gentle. As far as I
remember, he never even raises his voice at us.

An old photograph reminds me of a warm day in
late spring or early summer. It's a picture of my
mother sitting in the garden, holding my chubby
infant sister on her lap, and me standing next to
them. I have a scarf wrapped around my ears, for I
have the mumps. In my mind, I see other people.
Among them are Oma and my aunts, my father's
sisters, Tante Käthe and Tante Dora. All females

crowd around the baby and do the fussing and adoring that comes with the territory, and when they're done with that, they turn to me, pat my head, give me pitying looks and tell me how sorry they are that I'm sick.

I remember the sandbox not far from the house, on the kitchen side. This is not my favorite place to play. When the sand is dry, it feels funny on my fingers. In its wet state, it makes me dirty. I do not like dirt! But there's a long bench not far from it, right against the wall of the house, and I put pebbles on it. I place them in rows and count them. Soon my mother teaches me addition. As instructed, I count out three pebbles here and two pebbles there. Then I count them all together. One, two, three, four, five. Simple! Eva loves counting.

*

Vaguely, I recall a little brown dog. Her name - she's a female - is Mäuschen. *Maus*, in German, means mouse. Add the "chen," and it makes the mouse little. Therefore, Mäuschen stands for Little Mouse. Though the dog is small, she isn't quite as tiny as a mouse, but she's fast, always on the move, just like a mouse. She doesn't even want to lie down to let me stroke her. Perhaps she doesn't like children very much. My mother is often mad at her. Mäuschen takes off and has to be looked for in the neighborhood.

One day, my exhausted mother comes home, dragging our unwilling mutt by the leash, shouting something like, "Some kind of puppies this will be! Mäuschen got married to a St. Bernard. At the dump I caught them. And that huge dog stood over our tiny Mäuschen to protect her. He didn't want to let her come home with me."

How my mother has managed to put our bad, bad dog on the leash is as unknown to me as what it means for dogs to get married. Actually, I don't even remember seeing puppies.

I have a fairly clear picture of Muselchen, our tabby cat, cuddly and good-natured. I can still hear her purr. She's kid-friendly. Often, she doesn't finish her milk, and then Kater Murr comes around and laps it all up. To the last drop. Then he's so full and tired that he falls asleep right in front of the dish. He's a big, fat, white male cat, belonging to my Onkel Willi and my Tante Lotte, who live in the house in front of us. First he eats and drinks what he gets at his own place, and then he sneaks over to us to see what Muselchen has left. My mother laughs when she watches him. I crouch down on the floor near him and watch him, too. His lapping the milk gets slower and slower. One eye closes. He blinks with the other ... his little tongue gives a final lick. Now the second eyelid falls. His round head drops to the floor. Kater Murr is in dreamland.

We also have chickens. My mother has names for all of them. Sometimes, she calls, "Agathe! Beate! Renate!" That's all I can remember, and she sounds something like a chicken herself. Then her flock of feathered friends comes running and fluttering toward the wire-fence enclosure, making lots of real chicken noises while eagerly awaiting the grains of feed that will be tossed to them by their caregiver.

Sometimes, I'm allowed to go into the chicken coop with my mother, and then we come out with a number of eggs, which have to be handled with care so they won't break. Most are white, but some are brown, and my mother seems to like those best. We also have a rooster, who looks pretty, and he crows, "Kikirikiki!" That's German rooster language.

My Tante Lotte raises chickens, too. Hers are usually allowed to roam her garden, and they make a mess, even on the paths and in the driveway. I step gingerly. Chicken poop on my shoes or bare feet is not to my liking.

Unfortunately, we have to cross Onkel Willi's and Tante Lotte's backyard and use their driveway in order to get to the front gate. Our garden is part of my uncle's property. He has let my parents build their little house on it and live there until they are ready to erect a nice, big one on the lot they own on Fleischerstraβe, a bit closer to the center of town. But I don't know about all this until a few years later, when I'm older. Right now I'm only familiar with my pretty garden behind nice Onkel Willi's, located on Lauchstätter Weg in Rudow, a district of Berlin, Germany. And our cozy, little home seems just right to me.

Tante Lotte also has bunny rabbits. At least I think they are hers and not Onkel Willi's, because she's the one who takes care of them. The rabbits are in cages, one cage on top of the other, near the gate between the two gardens and right next to Onkel Willi's garage, in which he has two automobiles and a motorcycle. The bunnies are cute. I like it when they wiggle their noses. Sometimes, a grown-up lifts me up so I can be closer to the animals. Some are lazy and just lie in the back of their cage, probably too tired to hop around. Others are curious and come to the front, and they make little noises through their nostrils as if they want to sniff me. I can put my finger through the mesh and touch their tiny noses. Bunnies are really much more fun than chickens.

I like Tante Lotte, I think. On occasion, she can be funny. But I'm a lot fonder of Onkel Willi. He stops in to visit a lot, and when my mother, who is his younger sister, has something good to eat, she feeds him. He seems to enjoy her cooking very much, just like Kater Murr relishes Muselchen's milk. Only, Onkel Willi never falls asleep after his meal. He lingers quite a while, though, until my mother tells him, "You better go home now. Lotte will be mad at you." And then, when he has left, she mumbles something like, "If she would only take time to cook the food long enough. It's not surprising that poor Willi has stomach pains so often."

*

Onkel Willi always takes time to talk to Gisela and me. He likes to joke a lot. Actually, I remember him most clearly from the time I'm about four or five years old. Gullible me, I believe every word he says. Gisela, though two years my junior, appears to have a knack for looking through his fibs. Or is she too young to know what he's talking about and therefore ignores him?

Very clear in my mind is the time when my sister and I, after a little visit with Tante Lotte and Onkel Willi, are ready to go home and our uncle leads us to the door. I notice the holes in his old slippers. His toes are poking through, and I point at the openings, somewhat horrified.

"For ventilation," he explains. "My feet got too hot, and so I made holes to keep them cool. You should cut holes in your shoes, too."

I think it sounds like a great idea, though I would never dare to ruin my shoes that way. Gisela, however, gives him a look that seems to say, "Who are you trying to fool?" Then she turns away with an expression of utter disgust. Because Gisela gets easily irritated ... I think, Onkel Willi teases her more often. Off and on, he even snaps her pants or pulls them down, just a tiny bit, and then she gets very upset. He never does that to me.

Oh, Onkel Willi is quite a character! During the week, he has a job as printer for a major Berlin newspaper, the "Morgenpost." Opa, his dad, works there, too, but he's a typesetter. Both always suffer from toothaches, supposedly caused by the lead used in the printing process, and they chew tobacco to lessen the pain. We are all used to their teeth being in gentle chewing motion and to bits of dark tobacco juice needing to be wiped from the corners of the mouth.

"Those poor men," the relatives say.

On Sundays, Onkel Willi doesn't have to go to work, and he spends many hours in his garage. He's constantly taking his cars apart, fixing this and that, and then he puts everything back together and seems pleased. He lets Gisela and me watch while he works, but he asks us to be careful that we don't fall over his tools or the car pieces strewn all over the floor. We step with exaggerated care, and then we stand at a safe distance. Neither do we want to be in our uncle's way, nor do we intend to get dirty. To stay clean has been drilled into us.

Every Sunday - at least it seems like every Sunday, Oma comes to visit. When she's ready to go home, we all walk her to the trolley stop. It's a big group, which includes my parents, Tante Lotte, Onkel Willi, Gisela, and me. We are all in our Sunday best, except for Onkel Willi, who regularly has to be called out of his garage, often from under one of his automobiles. He only wipes his hands before joining us and, much to the disgust of his spouse, insists on coming along in his old shoes and dirty work clothes. Tante Lotte is the only one who shows displeasure, and the rest of us have a good time on our half-hour trek over dirt roads to the main street of Rudow, where Oma will catch the trolley to Britz, the section of the city in which she and Opa live.

It is never mentioned that Onkel Willi should drive Oma home - or to the public transportation stop, in bad weather, at least. Does he ever use his jalopies? Are they only a hobby ... or a convenient means of escape from his wife, perhaps? I can only remember one ride with him, but this comes later.

Onkel Willi uses his motorcycle. He takes it to work, I think. Most likely, Tante Lotte accompanies him on little fun trips, for the cycle has a sidecar attached to it. I've seen Oma sitting in that sidecar. Oma loves to go for a spin. Off and on, when the cycle is parked behind the house, Onkel Willi lets Gisela climb in the sidecar, and I'm allowed to sit on the front seat. Then I pretend that I'm driving. When my cousin, Achim, who's about five years older than I am, happens to be around, which isn't very often, he gets the seat in front, and I have to take the back seat and hang on to him. We make motorcycle noises. That's fun, too.

Achim is the son of Tante Klärchen, my mother's older sister. Actually, her name is Klara, just like Oma's name is Klara. But she's Klara Kühn, and Oma is Klara Krause, wife of Selmar Krause. If Tante Klärchen has already been divorced from Karl, her supposedly very handsome, womanizing husband, I don't know. I've never seen Achim's biological dad, I believe, only his stepfather, years later.

*

19

Everybody must like our little house in the suburbs. Or they enjoy the country atmosphere. Or could it be my mother's cuisine? Perhaps it is the whole package. Anyhow, all the relatives from the city flock to us. Before they arrive, my mother washes the floors. An hour later, because she detects grains of dirt, she wipes again. When my father asks, why she's doing it, she answers, "Because there's too much sand outside, and it constantly comes into the house."

On ordinary Sundays, when it's not somebody's birthday or another celebration, either the people from my mother's side of the family drift in - and that happens most often, or those related to my father show up. When something important goes on, all appear at the same time. Then some of the furniture has to be moved out to make room for extra tables and chairs. Even with just the Krauses visiting, it gets pretty overcrowded around our round table. For lack of chairs, we sometimes use the ironing board, which makes a nice bench for little kids such as Gisela and me. My mother has to sit closest to the door so she can get out to the kitchen and the food. Whoever has a seat farther in is stuck there until the end of the meal when other people have left the table. There's no wiggling through for emergencies. But my mother's food tastes good no matter how awkward the seating arrangement, and her wonderful cakes and tortes win her many praises. Since nobody has heard of calories and high cholesterol yet, and

20

carbohydrate and sodium counters don't exist, our family members happily stuff in the home baked goodies until their stomachs can't hold another bite. And there isn't a single fat person in the bunch!

When coffee time is over, the dishes are cleared away, and the weather isn't nice enough to enjoy the outdoors, the whole gang remains in the house. Let Tante Käthe, Tante Dora, perhaps Onkel Martin, who's my father's younger brother, and *Großer Opa*, translated Tall Grandpa, be there, then it means a lot of conversation will follow, which is quite boring for my sister and me. But we don't have to hang around. We have our toys, and we can very well occupy ourselves until it's time for the next meal, supper.

With only the Beetz family visiting - my father is Kurt Beetz; his dad is Richard Beetz, the tall grandfather, and he lives in Berlin-Britz like Oma and Opa - we don't need the ironing board. Then my mother has it easier, too, because she doesn't have to serve so many trays of all those delicious open-faced sandwiches, which consist of good, dark, German bread or crusty, white rolls covered with sweet butter, all sorts of tasty lunchmeats, and various delectable cheeses. Those crusty rolls are a Berlin specialty, but I don't realize this until many years later.

As a rule, my mother also serves potato salad, which, in Berlin, is prepared with mayonnaise and not with oil and vinegar like in the southern parts of Germany.

I am used to the Sunday commotion, but my little sister, apparently, prefers peace and quiet. I will never forget this scene: The door has barely closed behind the Beetz gang. Gisela stands in front of the huge mirror, which is part of our three-door closet. While crossing her hands over her chest, she gives an enormous sigh of relief and says, "*Glücklich*," meaning happy. She lets her head drop, so that her chin touches the collarbone, and when she looks up again, she studies her image in the mirror. She smiles. I assume she is satisfied with her grand performance.

Visits from the Krause bunch - my mother's name, before she got married, was Wally Krause - are livelier and definitely more entertaining. The Krauses all love to make music and sing. It is said, my uncles can play any instrument they get hold of, especially Onkel Willi. He always brings his accordion over to our house. Or, when he feels like it, he uses his squeezebox, fondly named *Knautschkommode* in German, which is a smaller version of the accordion and has to be squeezed in and pulled out a lot. Onkel Gerhard, much taller than Willi, his older brother, also owns and plays such instruments, but he doesn't bring them to our house very often, because that's a lot of carrying when he rides the streetcar and has the long walk across the fields to come to us. But he has his mouth organ in his pocket, and he gladly whips it out. Papa - that's my dad - plays the mouth organ, too. Achim knows how to blow the comb. When I try it, the tissue paper

22

covering tickles my lips. I don't even know how to whistle. I think all the others do, except for Gisela, who's too young for this. But what we all know is how to sing and laugh.

Those get-togethers are fun, and not even Gisela has to sigh afterwards.

*

The potato salad deserves another mention. Some of my aunts put bits of pickled or salted herring into their potato salads. Though my mother raves about those concoctions, she doesn't dare to serve them at our house. I wrinkle my nose at herring in salad. My dad, I think, is not fond of it either. And Gisela? She's such a picky eater that my mother worries about my sister's health. Her favorite nourishment seems to be milk. I could do without milk. Gisela is pudgy. I am tall and skinny.

When my mother takes us to the doctor for a checkup, he doesn't show concern for my sister's state of health, but he suggests putting a brick on my head to slow down my growth. This man scares me. If I had a choice, I would never go back to him again.

*

For a while, I'm afraid of my mother. Why? She always reads to us at bedtime. Sometimes, my father reads to us, too. Most of their stories are wonderful, but some of the Grimm's fairy tales are frightful. I especially recall *Der Machandelbaum*, the one about the cruel stepmother who kills the little boy, cuts him into pieces, cooks him, and then serves him as stew to his dad. His younger sister, Marleneken, wraps the bones into a silken cloth and lays them under a juniper tree. The bones turn into a beautiful bird that then sings his tragic song over and over again. In the end, after the bad woman reaps her just reward, the bird, miraculously, is transformed back into the little boy. I am terribly worried that my own dear mother might take a kitchen knife and do away with my sister and me. So I force myself to lie awake, and I listen to the noises that come from the kitchen where my mother is still doing things, and I hope she'll soon go to bed and stay there.

Mama, as Gisela and I call her, is really a very good mother. She's a gentle person - except when she's stressed out about something or tired of putting up with whatever naughtiness we come up with. Of course, I never believe I deserve the swat I'm getting from her. Off and on, I do get punished for something that is Gisela's fault.   Honestly!

The rule in our house is: DO NOT FIGHT. DO NOT HIT. That's not always easy. In general, my sister and I play very well together. But, since I'm the oldest, I sometimes dictate what should be done. When Gisela is not in agreement, she gets mad. Since she's not allowed to raise her voice at me or use her little fists, she "accidentally" steps on my foot to hurt me. And when she gets really, really mad, she hisses, "Z…i…e…g…e," in my direction, which, translated, means goat. The longer drawn out that word is, the better she likes it. And it's always in a low enough voice so my mother can't hear it. Real curse words are not in our vocabulary. Even as I get older, I remain a *"Ziege"* when Gisela gets upset with me. Said correctly, with the ultimate of feeling, the word sounds so wonderfully mean. Her stomping on my feet gets harder with age, especially when she wears those sandals with wooden soles, which are so popular during World War II. When I cry, "Ouch!" and glare at her, she gives me that innocent look and says, "Sorry. I didn't mean it." Of course, I don't believe a word she's saying. By the time she reaches age six or so, I think, she has outgrown this revenge tactic.

*

Now back to the spring of 1936. We are all going to Onkel Gerhard's wedding. He's marrying a woman named Gertrud, and the celebration takes place in the rural part of Landeck, quite a distance away, east of Berlin, where her parents own a farm. Landeck's nearest city is Schneidemühl, which is situated near the border of Pomerania and West Prussia. (After World War II, this part of Germany has become Polish.) I cannot recall if we travel by train or perhaps ride with Onkel Willi in his car. Oma and Opa go to the wedding, and my mother, Gisela and I, too. What about Tante Lotte? I don't remember.

Neither do I come up with a picture of my father at this festive occasion. Most likely, he stays at home to tend his store.

Oh, it's going to be fabulous! A true country wedding, lasting three days! Or even longer, according to our soon-to-be aunt's bragging. The grownups have been talking about it a lot. Everybody appears so excited. Do I like this Gertrud? I have no impression of her yet.

Here is what I remember about our stay in Landeck: On the morning of the wedding, we process, on foot, from the farm to the church, with the bride and groom leading the way and the guests following. Gisela and I wear beautiful, white, long-sleeved dresses, sown by my mother, the professional dressmaker. No other children have party clothes as pretty as ours. I am a bit worried that my new patent leather shoes might get dirty, because the road, which seems to be the main artery through the village, is somewhat muddy. It is also uneven with ruts from wagon wheels. I'm used to dirt roads that go across fields, and we have enough of them between town and the development where I live. I'm also familiar with cobblestone pavements in old Rudow, and with smooth surfaces of modern city streets and sidewalks. But here we are in true farm country, where people, animals, and horse-drawn wagons share one wide lane. Nothing is that bumpy at home. I'm also not used to people coming out of their houses to gawk at us. Of course now, decades later, I see nothing wrong with it. People love to see a bride and a groom. It makes them happy. And, really, in a small place like Landeck, how often does the spectacle of a wedding procession come the villagers' way?

I do not remember the church ceremony. Zeroing in on the wedding feast at the house is easy, though. Platters heaped with various kinds of meat, bowls filled with potatoes and assorted vegetables and who knows what other delicacies stand on the tables in the big room, and I'm hungry and eager to sit down right next to my mother. Let the food be served! But, to my great disappointment, all children are being herded into a small, narrow room, and Gisela and I don't know any of the other youngsters. They are probably all familiar with each other, for they trade jokes and laugh and giggle. Off and on, they are a little unruly. They pay no attention to my lost-looking sister and me. Finally, a woman brings our food. It looks nothing like what has been set out for the adults in the main dining area. It doesn't even taste good. "Rabbit stew," somebody says. A few kids refuse to eat it, and they also sneer at the one choice of vegetables that's on the plate. One boy opens the window and dumps his food over the side. A few others do the same. Gisela and I would never dare to participate in such naughtiness.

We anxiously wait to be released from our prison, but no adult comes to even check on us. I'm far from happy. If this is called a wedding celebration, they can keep it. Our family gatherings in Berlin are much

27

more fun. Also, the food at home is a hundred times better than this so-called feast.

Eventually, my mother comes to see how we are doing. "Stick it out a little longer," she says. "I'll come for you as soon as I can." Oh how the minutes and hours drag when you feel miserable!

Only one more thing about this adventure in Landeck comes to mind, and the more often it gets retold, the funnier it appears. Our Berlin family, all early risers, sits in the big country kitchen, waiting for the host family to get out of bed. We are hungry, but no breakfast is coming. My mother and Oma wash loads of dirty dishes from the day before. We pick up trash and sweep the floor. Still, nobody else stirs in the house. We get restless.

Suddenly, Tante Gertrud's mother bursts into the kitchen and announces, "The cow has to be milked." She runs in and out of the kitchen numerous times, always shouting the same thing, "The cow has to be milked!" It seems the poor cow gets as much attention as we, the guests. None.

Then my mother whispers to Oma, "We've already done everything else here, but we won't milk the cow for her, too."

"What about the three-day celebration?" somebody asks.

Big shrugs. Raised eyebrows. Mumbling. Grumbling. Some laughter.

And with the festivities apparently all fizzled out, we return to Berlin. It's so good to be back home again!   Home is the place I like best.

*

Summer arrives. The days turn hot. Just resting in the shade would be nice. But my mother has to drag us into town to do some shopping - every morning, before the sun rises too high in the sky. Gisela is lucky. She gets to ride in her stroller. I have to walk, half an hour, at least, each way, over parched, dusty roads. My poor mother sighs. The load she pushes is heavy, and the heat makes her sick.

"Why did we ever have to move to Rudow?" she whines. "This awful air in the summer here, I can't tolerate it! I can't breathe! I never suffered like this when living in Britz."

Every day except on Sundays, when the shops are closed, we have to go for fresh supplies. Since there is no refrigeration, and we don't even have blocks of ice, things would spoil if kept too long. Most of our purchases come from the stores in town or, on market days, from the vendors in the street.

I enjoy market days best, because there's so much to see. Fruits and vegetables are piled high on wooden tables, and more is stored in baskets that rest on the cobblestone pavement. Beautiful flowers are for sale ... more varieties than in our own garden ... or in Tante Lotte's ... and we really do have a lot. There's the pickle man, and I'm happy when my mother fishes a nice, plump, sour pickle out of one of his tall barrels and buys it for me. When I bite into my crunchy, dark green treat, the juice splashes out

29

and trickles down my chin. I love sour pickles right from the barrel.

The displays of sweets don't interest me very much. If I want candy, I can always get it from my father, who sells it in his store, together with ice cream on a stick or in a cone, tobacco wares, newspapers and magazines. Actually, it's not a real store, but a kiosk with a window through which he hands the goods to the customers. If they want to, they can also come through his door to make their purchases, but they're always in too much of a hurry, and so they use the window. Since my dad's place is right at a trolley stop, he caters to the commuters before they board the streetcar or when they get off. And on the other side, across the street, is the sports stadium. Athletes and fans make good patrons, too, especially when the soccer games are being played.

"Papa is his best customer," says my mother, and then she laughs. "He eats too much of his chocolate inventory." Actually, she consumes a pretty good amount herself. When something is offered to me, I often decline. "I'll save it for later," I say. I guess I rather eat a pickle from the market place.

Only on rare occasions, my mother buys a few items from the little corner store a bit down the road from our house, to the right. It's something like a convenience store. And when, unexpectedly, Mama's former coworker comes to visit with her awful son, we quickly walk to the bakery. This store is actually only a few hundred feet behind us, but, since all properties are surrounded by fences, we have to go down our street first, in the opposite direction from where the little store is, then make one turn, then another, and, finally, we come to this wonderful bake shop, where the aroma of fresh bread and cakes and cookies wafts through the air and pleasantly tickles my nose. I especially love the huge shortbread cookies that have big, sweet, buttery crumbs on one half and rich, dark chocolate on the other. If it weren't for that occasional cookie, I would've disliked putting up with the little stinker of a boy even more. Strangely, I neither remember his name nor what has been so terrible about him.

One thing is very nice about the hot season. We have a summer tub! It's a big, long, galvanized tub that stands on four little metal feet, and it has a handle on each side. When not in use, it is stored in the shed, which is attached to our house, toward the back, on the bedroom side. That's where the wood and the coal and the garden tools have their places, too. And where the porcupine hides some time later, which my mother mistakes for a brush. She picks it up, remarking, "Why hasn't Kurt put it where it belongs?" and then, immediately after, she lets out a scream, because that "brush" has pricked her.

Anyhow, we are so very, very lucky to have this tub, and I gladly help drag it from the shed into the garden. My mother wipes off the dust first, and then she scours it. I also do some wiping, for I'm eager to get our private "spa" into operation. Gisela, too, can hardly wait. Even if she's only two years old, she knows what a tub is for. A smaller, oval one is always filled up for us at bath time in the kitchen. When we sit in it, we are not allowed to splash. It would be bad to let the water slosh onto the floor.

Once the big bathtub is clean, the hardest job begins. It has to be filled with water. For that, my mother has to go to the well, located near Onkel Willi's house, and pump the water up by hand. Then she carries it, bucket after bucket after bucket, to the tub in our garden. So much water is needed! Poor Mama, she gets too exhausted and has to stop.

In the meantime, Gisela takes off her clothes ... and climbs in ... in the nude. Little kids and nakedness go together - at home as well as on public beaches. Europeans see nothing wrong with it. If my sister even owns a bathing suit at this tender age, I cannot recall.

The freshly poured water must've been very, very cold, but I can still see Gisela frolic in it. She whoops. She splashes. She slides back and forth, on her belly first, and then on her back, and her blond, curly hair fans out like streamers from her head.

As soon as my father comes home from work, he helps load the tub with more water. Then we all cool off in our private "swimming pool," usually two at a time. Bathing as a trio works, too. For fun, we try all four of us, crunched together, but one grownup, my father, who takes up the most room, quickly has to get out. Really, the tub is too small for so many people, and the precious water spills over.

Come to think of it, I probably don't wear my bathing suit all the time, either. But when

 Achim visits, I put on my suit or, at least, a pair of little panties.

*

   The Olympic Games are being held in Berlin, in the summer of 1936. My parents go to watch, perhaps on opening day, and they take me along. We sit in the stadium, on one of the higher tiers, and some athletes are running. I'm not even certain if this is the actual competition that's going on down there or a preliminary thing. What really makes an impression on me is the huge parade on the field, all those people marching to music and swinging colorful flags. Lots and lots of balloons are being released. They are flying up and up, and none comes to me so I can catch it. To hold a balloon in my hand would be heavenly. At least, I would have something to do while my mother and father are talking about sports and who should win. Of course, they are interested in sports events, because they've both been amateur athletes since their teens, just like all their sisters and brothers, and this is where they've met and fallen in love. I've heard the stories often.

   When the amusement park opens in Rudow, I believe I've found my athletic ability: horseback riding. Oh, what a joy! I pick the prettiest, the tallest stallion on the carousel, and I can hardly wait for the music to start, which signals the beginning of the ride. Around and around we go, and I wave to my parents. I'm sure they're very, very proud of me for

33

pushing so hard to make my horse go up and down. Of course, the more effort I put into it, the faster the merry-go-round turns. When I tell Mama and Papa about it, they nod and let me enjoy my imagined achievement. All the other rides I'm allowed to sample are, in my opinion, baby stuff. They are for little tots like Gisela. Give me a horse, and I'm happy!

*

I believe 1936 is the year when I start Sunday school. A young woman a few houses down the street from us is my teacher. In the beginning, she picks me up, and we walk together to the small building an endlessly long block to the left from us and then around the corner to the right, near the place that sells coal and firewood. The Protestant church, in which I've been baptized, *Rudower Dorfkirche* (Village Church of Rudow), is located in the old part of town near the street where the open market is always being held. The small place I go to now is a satellite worship center, convenient for the people in our area. I think hearing the Bible stories and learning some verses is nice, but getting acquainted with so many beautiful songs is the biggest fun. I love to sing, and I'm a fast learner. My teacher is amazed that I can always find the page for "A Mighty Fortress Is Our God" in my hymnal even though I don't know how to read yet. That's my secret. A red cherry stain is next to the page number.

Gisela likes to sing, too, and she does well for a girl of not yet three. At times, she has the words wrong, but that doesn't matter. We are very proud of her, even though we get the giggles when the text comes out really funny.

It is not surprising that we children are familiar with lots and lots of songs, for my mother has the radio going for hours on end, and she always warbles along. She seems to know every hit, tune and the words. And Gisela and I know all the children's songs.

My dad claims he can't sing. Actually, he has a very pleasant voice. Off and on, he tells us the story from his school days.

"We were practicing a song, and the teacher, Herr Probst, didn't like my rendition. So I changed my voice and sang real high, trying to please him. 'What is that?' screeched my horrified, old teacher, and then he made me sit down."

We like to listen to this tale, because Papa always gives us a sample of that funny, high-pitched singing. It is so hilarious.

*

Gisela turns three at the end of March 1937, and the relatives assemble for her birthday party. It is a beautiful spring day and warm enough for everyone to be outdoors to watch Gisela try out her new scooter and to cheer her on as she rides it from the patio down our garden path, past Tante Lotte's rabbits and Onkel Willi's garage, halfway around our uncle's and aunt's house, and then down the driveway to the big gate by the street. In my opinion, this beautiful, shiny, new scooter is too big for my little sister. In all fairness, it should be mine. Honestly, I can't understand why Tante Käthe has given that scooter to Gisela. She already owns one. She has that little, yellow, wooden one. It is simple, but still quite serviceable. And now she has been given this absolutely gorgeous, colorful one made of metal. It even has streamers hanging from its handlebars! To make matters worse, Gisela also owns a small tricycle, and I have not a single riding toy to my name. It's absolutely unfair! I am, as you might say, green with envy. But when I pout and complain to my mother, she simply says, "You can always share."

To my great surprise, Gisela rides her new scooter over to me, stops and asks, "You want a turn?" Of course I do, and as I push off and then seem to fly along the path, all my hurt evaporates.

Soon Onkel Willi begs to try out the new toy. Willingly, Gisela lets him have it. But Onkel Willi is quite a bit taller than a child, and he has to stoop to hold on to the handlebars. What a sight! The way he's bent down, he looks like a monkey. Kick, glide, kick, and glide … he turns the corner and heads for the gate … and everyone is laughing at his comical performance.

Since my sister and I are used to sharing, no further mention is made of her having three "vehicles" to her name while I own none. Sometimes she takes the big scooter and I make do with the little one. Then we switch. Or she rides the tricycle while I operate the new, shiny scooter. Together, we go on imaginary trips, either to visit our grandparents or to some made-up, far away place. Off and on, when we reach the front gate, we pause extra long to check if, by chance, a neighbor might walk by to notice the new toy. Just like we parade to the front in hopes that somebody catches a glimpse of our occasional new dresses. I don't recall that anybody has ever looked our way with special interest.

Six days after Gisela's birthday, on April 5, it is my fifth birthday. And what is my present from my parents? A bicycle. A two-wheeler! Red. What a beauty! I can hardly believe it. Gisela shows no sign of jealousy, and she doesn't even ask for a ride. I assume she realizes that she wouldn't be able to reach the pedals, anyhow.

Actually, it's pretty scary to sit so high up, especially when the bicycle wiggles in a dangerous way and threatens to tip over and toss me to the hard ground. If I want to learn how to ride this thing, I have to trust my father that he doesn't take his hand off the bike. He has his safety hold in back of me, right there by the saddle. I should be secure.

"Come on now, don't forget to pedal," he urges. "As long as you keep going, the bicycle will stay up."

And so I push. Right leg, left leg, right, left, on and on, faster, faster, learning the rhythm, until, suddenly, something doesn't seem quite right. Papa isn't as close as he has been in the beginning. I have to check. I turn my head. I forget to pedal. Oh no, the bicycle begins to teeter! I'll fall for sure. But my dear dad is near enough to catch me, and all is well.

"See, you can do it," he praises me. Then he teaches me how to apply the brake and jump off without falling.

After a few more practice sessions, I ride my bike like a pro. Now I'm ready to accompany my father on his early morning Sunday route, when he delivers newspapers to a few customers in our immediate neighborhood. We only go around one big block, and the whole trip doesn't take very long. It's fun riding with Papa. The only time I'm not so very happy is when he suddenly pedals too fast, keeps gaining on me and disappears around the corner. I have no idea why he leaves me behind like this, and I'm a bit scared. So I go as speedy as I can ... I reach the corner ... I make my turn ... and there he is, waiting for me. He laughs, but I don't think it's so very funny. By the time we reach home, all is forgiven.

"Why do you go to the trouble of taking the papers to those people?" my mother sometimes asks.

"They are my regulars, and when they can't pick up the newspaper on their way to work on Sunday, I bring it to them. It makes for good relations, and I don't mind."

That's my dad, always trying to please. I wonder why Mama is a bit harsh with him. But being so young, I don't realize yet that grownups can get irritated when they are overwhelmed with a project, could use a helping hand, and the other person doesn't give it, but, instead, runs off to do favors for strangers. In my eyes, Papa is the big, strong hero who can do no wrong. I feel bad when he gets criticized.

*

One day, my mother takes Gisela and me to a garden show somewhere in Berlin, possibly at the exhibition center by the *Funkturm* (radio tower). There, we receive samples of a new variety of tiny tomatoes, advertised as *Zuckertomaten*, meaning sugar tomatoes, known in the United States as cherry tomatoes. My sister, the finicky eater, loves them. From then on, when our old- fashioned tomatoes in the garden ripen, my mother selects the smallest ones and gives them to Gisela. "Here is another *Zuckertomate*," she says. Little Gisela gets fooled every time. She pops those tiny tomatoes into her mouth ... and is pleased. I would like to laugh but know better.

Lots of things grow in our garden. Besides the tomatoes, beans are planted in neat rows, and lettuce and Swiss chard. Early in the year, my mother also grows peas and radishes. I do remember a clump of chives near the kitchen door. Parsley is always present, because my mother loves to decorate her potato salad with it. "It gives a nice touch of color," she says. I never eat the green sprigs, and if anybody else does I don't know.

Several gooseberry and currant bushes are to the left of the vegetable plot. A space for flowers, perennials, is in that corner, too.

In my opinion, our garden looks prettiest in May, around Mother's Day. That's when the lilacs are in bloom. Imagine! We have three sides of our property surrounded by those tall bushes. The fragrance of lilac blossoms is intoxicating. All along the fourth side, which is the one where our garden abuts Onkel Willi's, sprawl various kinds of ornamental shrubs, pretty big in size. At least two of those giants produce white berries in late summer. We are not allowed to eat the berries, but we can step on them, and then they make a nice little exploding sound. *Knallbeeren* we call them - bang berries.

In the open space in front of the gooseberries and the currants, which is on the bedroom side of the house, stands a chestnut tree with a table under it. Perhaps, it is only a bench, because Gisela wouldn't dare to jump off a table. But this doesn't occur until a bit later. Or would she jump from the height of a table? She might, this little daredevil.

Alongside the walk to the right, are flowers and a few trees. But the main attraction, definitely, in the open space on that side, is the gym set, which has a wooden board for regular swinging, and a bar and rings for doing gymnastics. Gisela, if she wants to soar way up into the air and then screech with delight, still needs an adult to push her. I, of course, am already big and strong to go high and higher all by myself. I love the bar and the rings, and I do all kinds of fancy exercises on them. At least, I consider them fancy.

*

Suddenly, my mother approaches me with a strange idea. She wants to send me to ballet classes. "You would have to practice at home, faithfully," she explains.

My protest is instant and vehement. No! Classes I can tolerate, but no practicing in front of Mama and others. All the visiting relatives would probably want to see what I've learned. Forget it! I'm too shy.

Strangely, my mother never brings the subject up again until many years later, when I'm all grown and have daughters of my own, who gladly take dance lessons. "I've always dreamed of dancing ballet myself," she confides, "and now let me help you pay for the girls' training."

*

The unexpected happens. Onkel Willi comes over and asks, "Do you want to go for a ride in my car?"

He wants to drive all the way to the Spreewald, which is an area a few hours south of Berlin.

I've seen the Spree before, but only where it runs through the city, somewhere near the famous *Brandenburger Tor* (Brandenburg Gate) and the imposing government buildings, which have all those statues of naked people in front. The river isn't very wide, but it is deep enough to let boats bring goods into Berlin. Mama says, "That's why we are lucky to be able to buy fresh fish here. People in many other German cities are not as fortunate. No river – no boats – no fish. Some folks never get to see fresh fish. How awful!"

Though I do eat my fish when it's served, I can't say it's my favorite food. A good pork chop or a crispy chicken leg I could drool over, but fish … with tiny bones in … it's nothing to get too excited over. That's my opinion.

Anyhow, now I'm curious to find out what the Spreewald looks like. And to take a ride in the car with Onkel Willi … wow! Thank God, my mother says, "Yes, we'll come along." She could've also answered, "Sorry, Willi, but we've other plans for today."

Gisela is hopping around with glee. She can't wait to get going.

Tante Lotte isn't coming along. She only holds the big gate open for us and then closes it behind the automobile.

At first, I wonder why she doesn't want to join us, but I soon find out the reason. Oma will be picked up, and that's why we have the empty passenger seat. With a tight fit, of course, we could've put Tante Lotte in the back seat, where Mama, Gisela and I are sitting. But if she prefers to stay home, let her. I have no time to worry about her, because there are too many things to look at and to digest in my mind.

Berlin, in 1937, does not have much traffic. Very few people own a car. They walk, ride bicycles, or take public transportation. When Onkel Willi's jalopy zips by, the walkers soon disappear in the distance. The bicyclists stay behind, too. Since trolleys have to stop frequently to take on passengers and to let them off, they have no chance to keep up with us. But even without their stops, they would be slower than my uncle's car. Off and on, I spot a sleek, shiny automobile that looks a lot newer than the one we are riding in, but who cares? A car is a car, as long as it keeps rolling and takes us somewhere.

A few trucks are on the road, also, and we even pass some horse-drawn wagons. Why aren't the horses afraid of motorized vehicles that go by so very fast and make noise? Horses don't seem to care. If waiting by the curb for their owners to return, they keep on munching their oats or closing their eyes as if asleep.

When we get to Britz, Onkel Willi parks his car in front of the apartment building, and then he goes upstairs to inform Oma that we have arrived. If she has any knowledge of this trip to the Spreewald, I don't know. Onkel Willi may have talked it over with her, perhaps on his way home from work. He always has to go in that direction, anyhow. But if Oma has no inkling of this outing, and it's as much of a surprise to her as it has been to us, she certainly gets ready in a great hurry. Honestly, she comes down with Onkel Willi in no time at all. She loves to go for a ride, be it in an automobile or the sidecar of the motorcycle. Perhaps, the back seat of the motorcycle is even better to her liking than the safer sidecar. Yes, Oma loves excitement. Even when it comes to riding the roller coaster or the Ferris wheel at the amusement park, she's the one who seems to have the most fun.

Naturally, Oma is happy to see us all, and we're glad she's coming along. And after she's all settled in the front seat, we're off on our adventure.

In no time at all, we're out of Berlin and on tree-lined country roads. We pass woods and meadows and little villages and towns. Nothing of real interest happens until, suddenly, Onkel Willi declares that his directional signals aren't working properly. "Can you help me out, girls?" he asks.

"Sure," we answer.

"When I say, 'right,' Gisela has to reach out her window and lift up the arrow until we've turned the corner. When I say, 'left,' you do the same on your side, Evchen. Do you know what I'm talking about?"

Gisela jumps off her seat, ready for action. I lean forward, waiting for my first task. Let the fun begin! And as soon as Onkel Willi calls out his intended left or right turns, we flick our assigned arrows up and

44

down as needed. I guess it's good that he has us along.

Eventually, we come to the area called Spreewald. It's a rather pretty place with lots of canals, on which the people row their boats to get themselves and their harvests from one place to another. But we have to stick to the narrow road that winds alongside the waterways. I remember the Spreewald as being very green, shady, and smelling of water. In the fields, the cucumbers are growing. Cucumbers seem to be everywhere.

"This is where the famous pickles come from," explains Oma, and then we stop to buy some. Yum! I'm a pickle lover, anyhow.

In a quaint souvenir shop, Oma buys herself a little, wooden rowboat with two tiny porcelain dolls sitting in it, a boy and a girl. They are dressed in the fancy costumes of the area. Two wooden oars come with the set. It's such a pretty memento. Gisela has it now, since Oma is gone, and she treasures it.

*

Toward the end of the year, we go to an open house at one of the radio stations. All young visitors are encouraged to sing along with the "Kunterbunt" kids, the ones who are regulars on a children's program. Gisela and I are quite willing to participate, for we love to sing, and we know all the songs from always listening to the program. And now, oh how exciting, we can actually sit in a semicircle together with those young radio stars whose names we know so well! This is so exciting. It is the biggest fun. I feel right at home. Unfortunately, the heavenly time comes to an end much too quickly, and the nice woman in charge, the one who calls herself Kunterbunt, shakes hands with all her young guests and thanks them for their participation.

Shortly after, a letter arrives in the mail, inviting me to become a regular on the radio show. My mother is excited, and because I seem to be willing to sing with the other kids at the studio, she fills out the necessary acceptance forms and returns them to Kunterbunt. But, as fate will have it, I do not become a radio singer.

"Kunterbunt writes, you are too old," explains my mother. "Since you'll be six soon and ready for first grade, it wouldn't pay to get you started with the show. They only want children who don't go to school yet."

I think my mother is more disappointed than I am.

*

The winter goes by, and then, suddenly, my first day of school arrives. Like all the other beginners, I'm being walked to school. I proudly carry my brown leather bag on my back and the big, beautiful, colorful, cone-shaped container called *Schultüte* in my arm. It's tradition! Every child has to have such a cone, about twenty-four inches high, and filled with goodies to sweeten the first day of classes. But I'm

46

not allowed to peek yet to see what's hidden inside, under the silky paper, tied with a pretty ribbon. Only after school lets out can the ribbon be removed.

First, all new students, with mothers, fathers, little sisters and brothers by their sides, have to assemble in the schoolyard by the flagpole. We suffer through a long, boring ceremony. Kids fidget. Some little ones really fuss, and a few escape their parents to amuse themselves on the gym equipment a few feet away. I guess Gisela would like to run over there, too, but my mother holds her by the hand. I know I have to be a good girl and stand still until dismissal.

The principal makes a speech. His opening sentence will always stick in my mind. "You will never forget the date of your first school day," he says, "because it is our *Führer's* birthday, April 20." On this day, in 1938, as far as I can remember, I sing Germany's national anthem for the very first time. I also have to raise my right arm for the "*Sieg Heil*," because everybody else is doing it, and Mama gives me a nudge to comply with what is expected. If my memory hasn't failed me, the next "*Sieg Heil*" from me doesn't come until four years later, during another ceremony.

Finally, the welcoming business is over, and a pleasant, young woman introduces herself as our teacher. With a big smile, she leads us to our classroom and assigns us a desk. In the beginning of the school year, I have a seat toward the front. Later, I get moved farther back, near the window. I guess she likes changes. If she has other reasons, I don't worry about them. All I care about is doing my work and not getting into trouble.

I really like my teacher … most of the time. Whoever gets all the spelling words or math problems correct is allowed to line up in front of the class to receive a tiny, round candy, called *Butterlinse.* Translated, it means butter lentil. This candy tastes so good … because it is earned.

As much as I like my teacher, I'm also a bit afraid of her, for one reason only. When a classmate raises his or her hand to ask to go to the bathroom, she always says, "Go, but you have to be back in five minutes." She checks the clock. Woe the kid that returns late! A tongue-lashing is certain, perhaps even a whack with the stick. I dread to have to ask to be excused. Why? The first graders are housed in a small addition to the two-storied, original school building, and they have to cross the schoolyard to get to the bathrooms in the big school.

Often, there's a line. So many older students are already waiting to use the facilities. By the time we little ones get our turn, too many minutes have gone by, and we are late getting back to class. I'm afraid of being punished. I hate humiliation.

So, one day, I really, really have to go, but I try to hold it. No luck. I soil my pants badly. It stinks. Nobody says a word. Unfortunately, this happens to be a day on which my mother is going to pick me up from school, for we have to quickly take the trolley into Berlin for some important reason.

School lets out. Feeling terribly uncomfortable with that load in my pants, I meet my mother. There's no stopping my tears.

She knows what it's all about. She smells it right away. To my great relief, she doesn't act mad, just frustrated.

"We have to get you cleaned up before we can go anywhere," she says. "Come!" Then she takes my sister by the hand, and I follow. We stop at a nearby store that sells underwear and sundry things, and she makes me stay outside - for good reason, and she buys me a new pair of panties. Then we walk to the brook that runs by the next corner. Fortunately, a few bushes grow by the side of that brook, and I can hide behind them while my soiled piece of clothing is being removed and I'm getting cleaned up with lots and lots of cold water. After that, my mother rinses my stinky panties, wrings them out, and stuffs them into a bag. She takes those wet ones along on our trip. She wouldn't leave a perfectly good piece of clothing behind. It costs money, and she has to save her pennies.

In first grade, we use slates and graphite styles to do our schoolwork. When I work on my writing assignments at home, it takes me an eternity to fill my slate. Since I want each letter to be perfect, I move my style in slow motion. The slower the movement, the more uneven the letters appear, especially the Ss which, in German script, used in first grade, have an upward slanted first stroke, followed by a long downward one. I erase my bad letters with my sponge. Then I wipe the slate dry with a rag. Frustrated, I try again. Eventually, my mother sits down beside me and urges me to hurry up. Amazing! The faster I let my writing stick go up and down, the straighter are my letters. Gisela, when she enters school two years later, seems to know this trick right from the start. Her Ss stand like soldiers, all neatly lined up, beautiful white lines on the black slate. Lucky for Gisela - her no-fuss attitude pays off.

One day, my teacher announces a big contest, sponsored by a savings and loan association. Students are asked to make up a slogan that encourages saving, and then they have to draw a picture to go with it. I make a colorful crayon picture of a house and write, "Who faithfully saves can build a house."

Hooray! I win! A savings bond arrives in my name. What happens to the win? I honestly don't know, but I speculate my prize money remains in the account of that certain financial institution until it becomes worthless after World War II.

Apparently, my parents are very pleased with my first report card, and, as reward, they buy me a doll. She is the most beautiful doll I've ever owned. Her hair is dark brown, done up in braids, and her eyes, which have real lashes, open and close. I call her Inge.

*

October 20, 1938, is an important day. My parents have been married for ten years, and now they will celebrate their wedding anniversary. All relatives are invited to a big party at the house.

For many days, my mother is busy with housecleaning and cooking and baking. And then, on the day of the party, we have to go through all that commotion with the furniture. Extra tables need to be set up; the beds have to go. They probably get stashed in the small room off the entranceway, the one with the trapdoor to our little cellar. Onkel Willi comes over to help. Perhaps Großer Opa lends a hand, too. When everything is set up, and the tables, pushed together in one long row, are covered with our best table linens, and china and silverware are in place, Mama brings in the flowers. Honestly, it looks very festive.

Soon, the guests arrive. Onkel Martin, baker and fine candy maker by trade, brings two fancy tortes. One is covered with orange slices, another with banana. Both have whipped cream on top, and they look beautiful, like real pieces of art.

"Thank you, Martin," my mother says. "But really, you shouldn't have."

Onkel Martin seems very proud of his creations.

The big meal my mother serves is delicious. Nobody is too shy to partake heartily. The grownups drink wine. *Zellers Schwarze Katze*. I know, because even years later, my mother still talks about it.

"Papa and I went to select the wine and told the dealer we wanted exactly the kind we'd just tasted, from that specific year. What we had sampled was excellent. And then he sent us sour wine. He cheated us." Oh, Mama remains mad until the day she dies. Almost.

When dessert is being served, my mother's tortes disappear first. Everybody always raves about her beautifully decorated butter cream tortes. Some prefer the chocolate creams, others the vanilla. I like both equally well, I think. Mama's marble cake, as a rule, is also well liked, but I'm not sure she has baked it for her anniversary. It may have been something else, something equally good. She has so many delicious recipes.

Later, Mama gleefully announces, "See, my tortes disappeared before Martin's." Such rivalry! It seems my uncle can never outdo my mother.

When the Beetz and Krause families celebrate, it is always a time filled with laughter, music making and singing. On this happy occasion, the jubilation goes on until well into the night. It tires me out, and I believe Gisela has already fallen asleep in some corner. So, when the guests have finally disappeared, after having assisted with the changeover from dining hall to bedroom again, I'm all too glad to fall into bed and drift off to dreamland.

*

To give a better picture of our house, I should perhaps mention that our living room and bedroom are just one big space with no wall separating the two areas. It is heated by an iron stove, round in shape, which sits on a flameproof slab and has a long stovepipe in the back that leads to the chimney. When a wood or coal fire roars in the burning chamber, my mother usually keeps a pot or a kettle with water on the flat top of that stove. Sometimes, she also places apples up there. Baked apples then fill the air with their tantalizing aroma, and they taste so delicious, especially, when served with a dash of cinnamon and a good sprinkling of sugar.

In the kitchen, we have the big, black, cast iron cooking stove. This one, at times gives my mother problems. It doesn't ventilate as well as the heating stove in the other room. Mama often gets mad at the wind when the fire doesn't want to cooperate and smoke blows into the kitchen. This is especially annoying when she wants to use the oven to bake a cake or to roast a goose or some other big piece of meat. Oh, she gets so frustrated then! Somehow, though, her culinary creations turn out just fine. Papa sings her praises all the time, and he gives her a kiss after every meal. I think my parents are the most loving and the very, very best.

Though I love my mother dearly, sometimes she gets me upset. Like when I find my stuffed dog in the kitchen stove one morning, ready to be set on fire. How is this possible? Mama admits her dastardly intention. Why does she want to kill my doggie?

"This stuffed thing is old, worn, dirty, and absolutely not worth having around," she tells me.

I'm outraged. I burst into tears. I put up a fight.

53

My mother apparently can't take my yammering anymore, and so she relents. The dog is taken out of the pit, cleaned of soot and ashes, and handed back to its owner, me. For a little while, my stuffed pooch gets more loving than it has seen in a long while. Do I care that its brown fur has lost its fuzz here and there? Does a missing eye make a difference? No! And the dirty spots don't count, either. How can Mama have been so cruel to even consider doing away with my dearest, longtime pal?

*

December. We expect an important visitor. St. Nicholas, who looks something like Santa Claus where we live, but apparently dresses in Catholic bishop's regalia in some other areas, according to pictures I've seen of him, comes to obedient children and rewards them with sweets. So, before going to bed on December 5, Gisela and I put our shoes by the door - only one each, for two would be greedy and displease the good, old man. Then, when we wake up the next morning, we find chocolate, marzipan, and, perhaps, also an apple in our shoes. Happiness reigns. Mama doesn't mind if we have some sweets before breakfast. She just doesn't want me to dawdle, because December 6 is not one of those official holidays that keep the schools from being open.

With St. Nicholas Day out of the way, Christmas approaches quickly. Soon, the house is filled with the most tantalizing, sweet aroma of cookies baking in the oven. My mother always creates hearts and stars and bells and a few other cut out, sweet delicacies for the holidays. Gingerbread, the famous *Nürnberger Lebkuchen*, she buys in the store. She also stocks up on sugar and chocolate wreaths, *Kringel*, and small, hollow chocolate balls, bells, and pinecones, which are wrapped in colorful foil. All those special goodies are for hanging on the Christmas tree. They are edible decorations.

Gisela and I cut strips of shiny, colored paper, and then we glue them into links to form long chains. They are our garlands for the Christmas tree.

From the girl across the street I've heard that she snoops around her house to find out what presents she and her siblings will get for Christmas. That's so stupid! Santa, in Germany known as *Weihnachtsmann*, doesn't hide gifts. He carries them all in his sack and delivers them, in person, on Christmas Eve. No wonder Mama doesn't like it when this girl, who is also my classmate, wants to play with me. She's bad, according to my mother, and nothing but trouble. She's destructive, uses bad language, and, oh horror! ... she dares to sass her own mother. In my opinion, the girl is not just bad, but she's also crazy.

One evening, however, by pure accident, while I'm looking for something in the closet, on the highest shelf, I come across a box that doesn't seem to belong there. Since I'm standing on a chair, it's easy for me to lift the lid and peek into that box. I allow myself only a very quick peek.

Oh my goodness, I can hardly believe it! There's a doll, and she looks exactly like my Inge, but she has medium brown hair, with a slight tint of red, instead of Inge's really dark tresses. Now I feel terribly guilty for having given in to my inquisitiveness, and I quickly climb down from the chair. *No word to anyone*, I think. But I keep wondering, why Santa would be hiding a doll in our closet. Perhaps, the girl across the street isn't quite as crazy as I think ... just bad like my mother says.

Our Christmas tree gets put up in the kitchen, on the little table in the corner. This is the table Gisela and I always use when we choose to play in the kitchen. It sits right next to the big table by the window. Though I know that other people have their tree in the living room, I see nothing wrong with ours being in the kitchen where we spend most of our time. Indeed, it looks very beautiful there.

We have white wax candles on our Christmas tree. Real ones. Each one is clipped to a little metal tray that is attached to a long rod, which is screwed into the trunk of the tree. Oh, it looks so festive when the candles are lit and the warm glow spreads over the strands of silver tinsel and makes them shimmer.

Each year, the pretty glass ornaments have to be admired anew. But more appealing than anything else on the tree are the sweet decorations that can be eaten. As soon as Mama or Papa says, "You may plunder the tree," there's no stopping my sister and me. This, of course, never happens before Christmas Day. It also doesn't mean we may "plunder" in excess, take all the chocolate and sugar candy ornaments at once. Moderation is in order.

Finally, our long-awaited *Weihnachtsmann* knocks at the door and asks to be let in. Though I've been informed by a few know-it-all kids in school that the good, old man with a beard, the one who visits children on Christmas Eve, is an impostor, and I should've, by now, being an intelligent child, wondered why our holiday guest always hides behind a false face, I've no doubt that this man is the true *Weihnachtsmann*.

I stand in awe. When he inquires, if I've been good, I nod. When he says, "Recite a Christmas poem," I obey. But why is he so very mean to my mother? Every year it's the same sad story. She recites her little verse quite nicely, and he still chides her for misbehaving. Then he gives her some whacks with the nasty switch he carries. Even if that tied-together bunch of small twigs is decorated with little bits of colored silk paper, it's no pleasure to behold.

Strangely, the gift-bearing visitor is never awful to my father, and I definitely cannot complain about the treatment he gives Gisela and me. Anyhow, I'm always relieved when the talking is done and it's time for all of us to sing Christmas carols. Of course, *Weihnachtsmann* sings along, and then it's exactly like our normal family get-togethers - cozy, heartwarming. Eventually, our night visitor opens his sack and distributes the presents, we thank him kindly for his generosity, admire what has been given to us, and then we sing some more. Sure enough, Gisela now cradles her new doll, the one I've already briefly caught a glimpse of a few weeks earlier. I have no idea how this *Weihnachtsmann* has managed to get the doll out of our closet and into his bag. It's probably part of the magic of Christmas.

The following day is spent with my maternal grandparents. All the other Krauses come, too. It's tradition.

*

Oma and Opa live on the second floor of a big apartment house, at the corner of Chausseestraße and Hannemann Straße. A grocery store, Kaisers (owned by A&P), a bakery, and Mars Funeral Home occupy the ground floor. Herr Mars, the owner of the funeral home, only sells the caskets and makes funeral arrangements. He handles no dead people. Sometimes, when the furniture is in complete disarray in my grandparents' place due to a big party, Oma jokingly declares she'll go downstairs and sleep in one of the caskets. Then everybody laughs.

Five families live on Oma's and Opa's floor. We have to knock at the second door from the right, the one by the inside corner, because that's my grandparents'. Sometimes, the bell works, other times, it doesn't. It seems to be temperamental. Oma usually opens the door or, when she's too busy in the kitchen at the moment, one of the early-arrived relatives lets us in.

"*Frohe Weihnacht!*" is the German greeting, accompanied by a lot of handshaking and, perhaps, a little hug. Our family is not much into hugging. Germans, in general, during those days, do not believe in embraces and kisses as part of saying hello or good-bye. Firm handshakes are the practice.

With the first greetings out of the way, we walk down the long hallway and into the kitchen where the fat goose is roasting in the oven and the rest of the holiday meal is cooking on the stove. Oma doesn't have a black, cast-iron stove like we have in our house. Hers is a big, tiled one, built right into the kitchen, against the wall. She also has running water and doesn't have to go downstairs to pump it, even though there's a pump on the sidewalk, visible from the bedroom window. I've never noticed anybody getting water from this huge, green pump with the enormous handle. "It's good for emergencies," somebody has once said. "And it can still be used to give horses a drink." This makes sense to me. Off and on, even in the city, horses come clip clopping along. If it happens to be a white one, my mother quickly calls out, "*Schimmel, mein Glück!*" It means, "White horse, my luck!" She has many sayings. Oma has them too. I learn new ones from them all the time.

My grandparents' kitchen is long and narrow. This is Oma's domain and the place where all the women congregate. When they're not helping with the food preparation or the dishes, they still sit or stand in there, talking and laughing.

Near the big cooking stove is the door that opens into the spacious living room. Hanging from the high ceiling is a beautiful crystal chandelier. To clean all those many dangling pieces, the prisms, takes hours, Oma says. She has to climb on a ladder to get to them.

In the far corner to the right is the tiled oven, which reaches from the floor all the way to the ceiling. It is beautiful.

By the outside corner of the room is a double door, and this leads to the balcony where, in the summer, Oma tends her geraniums. Gisela and I like this balcony, because, from there, we can watch so many interesting things that are going on in the streets. Chausseestraße is the main artery. The trolley goes cling clanging by. Off and on, a car comes along. Then a horse-drawn wagon appears either transporting goods or with a man trying to hawk his wares or picking up junk, which people want to get rid of. Of course, there are always people to watch, some in a hurry, others just out for a stroll, or kids playing. Hannemann Straße doesn't have a trolley, but the municipal offices and the fire station are across the street. On occasion, we can see the big doors open and the engines pull out. That's exciting! In Rudow, all is quiet … day and night. From our house and garden it's a rarity to even see a neighbor.

On this festival day, the most important spot in my grandparents' living room is the corner that has the Christmas tree. Oh, is this tree huge! It reaches from the floor almost up to the ceiling. And on it hang so many very, very old, beautiful ornaments, including several pretty glass birds with fancy, colorful tails. Of course, a tree that size holds more sweets than our much smaller tree at home, and we are always allowed to remove some goodies for immediate consumption. Gilded walnuts from ancient times hang in the branches, too, and when my mother dares to snitch one a few years later, and she cracks it open and tries to eat it, she has to spit it out again, because it tastes so horrible.

Opa is in the living room, sitting in his comfortable chair near the tree. Usually, his chair is in the corner, and in front of it is a small table on which he keeps his smokes, the chewing tobacco, and his playing cards. Because of the tree, his furniture has been pushed to the side. Of course, Opa is happy to see us, and I can still remember the twinkle in his eyes and the way one corner of his mustache goes up when he gives Gisela and me a friendly wink.

Gisela, Achim, and I usually play on the upholstered piece of furniture that's similar to a couch, which Oma calls a *Chaiselongue*, which is a French expression, and that *Chaiselongue* is on the other side of the room. Our favorite toys are in that corner, in a big, sturdy, wooden box. Unfortunately, my sister and I don't know how to play the old board games well. Perhaps Achim does, because he's so much older than we are, but I don't think he's interested in teaching us. What is extremely interesting to play with is the toy store, a fairly big contraption, made of wood, with all kinds of compartments and drawers that hold little boxes and a great variety of small items for sale. A scale to weigh out purchases is there, a cash register with a tinkling bell, and play money.

When we tire of buying and selling, we put everything back in its place and get out Oma's zither. This is a large instrument, which has pretty flowers painted on its shiny, black frame. With the help of music sheets, pushed under the strings, we are able to pluck out simple melodies. Even if it's not a feast to the ears, we like it. Of course, when Mama or Oma play the instrument, it sounds a lot better. My uncles are good at it, too, and they don't need those music sheets to guide them.

Just like the women stick to the kitchen much of the time and we, the small fry, amuse ourselves in that play corner, so have the men staked out the area near Opa as their territory. But when it's mealtime, everybody comes together and crowds around the long table set up in the center of the living room.

Oma's holiday food is delicious. The goose has a crisp skin, and the stuffing, which includes apples and prunes, is so yummy that I almost believe it's the best part of the whole meal.

Someone - it always seems to happen - asks, "Mother, did you cook rice pudding for dessert?"

Oma answers, with a dead-serious face, "No."

In chorus, her guests reply, "That's good."

"Why?"

"Because you burn it every time."

Oma shrugs and simply states, "It can't be helped. Rice pudding ALWAYS burns."

With that, the subject is dropped.

For the Christmas celebration, Oma has baked good crumb cake, her specialty.

When the feast is done, the table has been cleared, and food and drink have somewhat settled in the stomach, Onkel Gerhard excuses himself. He insists he needs a little walk to help his digestion. It's unbelievable! Every year, when he steps out for a while, *Weihnachtsmann* makes his Britz visit, and poor Onkel Gerhard never gets to see the good man.

Like the evening before, we go through the ritual of reciting our little verses and being rewarded with presents, and my mother, again, is getting punished with the switch for absolutely no reason at all. I'm just glad this mean, old fellow does not deny her the gifts marked for her. Though he seems to be annoyed that Onkel Gerhard is absent, as usual, he leaves things for him. Tante Gertrud sets them aside with the promise to hand them to her husband as soon as he returns from his ill-timed walk.

By the cozy light of the candles on the tree, we all sit together, talking, singing, laughing, and enjoying each other's company on this wonderful holiday. Does anyone have a foreboding that this might be the last Christmas the whole family will be together?

If the grownups already sense the inevitable coming of the war, they do not talk about it in front of the children. Only Opa and my uncles discuss politics, off and on, usually while playing cards, and when Onkel Willi gets too agitated, someone warns him to be quiet before he gets himself into deep trouble. I have no idea what they are talking about.

In Germany, Christmas is celebrated for two days, and both are legal, marked on the calendar. Easter and Pentecost, too, have two-day celebrations. While December 25 is pretty much for get-togethers with as many relatives as can be rounded up, the day after is mainly for the immediate family. Or people use it to go out of town to visit someone special - or to take in a show. Honestly, I can't remember if we spend the day alone, just Mama, Papa, Gisela, and I, or if the Beetz side of the family is showing up. This would be plausible, for they, too, would want to have a piece of Christmas with us and exchange presents.

*

In the spring of 1939, I enter second grade. Now, my classroom is in the old, big building, with the windows facing the street. Fräulein Wesenberg is my new teacher. She's already up in years, has gray hair, and she's on the tall side and a bit plump. If she would smile more often and act kinder, I could learn to like her. But no, she's strict and demanding, and she gets mad when some of her students don't understand immediately what she's trying to teach.

64

Am I glad I'm not one of the dumb ones! I think she would like to put some kids, especially a few boys, in the special education school. At a parent-teacher conference, she admits to my mother that she's not used to teaching young children. She's had upper classes in the past.

In second grade, we abandon the old German writing and learn *Kursivschrift,* cursive. Also, we now have to write on paper, in ink. And it has to be neat, without ink spots. Our desk has an inkwell, but I'm required to carry my own little bottle in my school bag, in case the well in my desk is empty. I also need a tiny rag for wiping my pen clean, and I must not forget the blotter to dry my writing before turning a page or closing my notebook. If I forget to blot, I'm in big trouble. Smudges make Fräulein Wesenberg mad and bring down the grade.

When we sing in class, I get irritated. Every song sounds like a dirge. So awfully slow! Sometimes, I try to inject some speed. Then I sing extra loud, with a little push. It doesn't work. To my great amazement, the teacher doesn't reprimand me. It is possible she's so enchanted with her own slow performance that she doesn't pay attention to me. One day, my mother passes our open windows and hears our singing. "You are right," she tells me later. "It does sound as if you are all going to sleep."

Fräulein Wesenberg teaches us a few things about good nutrition. The day I'll never forget is the one when breakfast is being discussed, especially the importance of drinking milk.

"Who didn't have milk this morning?" she asks.

I raise my hand. A few of my classmates put theirs up, too.

We, the guilty ones, have to line up by her desk, which sits on a platform.

"What did you drink for breakfast?" she inquires as I step up.

"Hot chocolate," I reply in a meek voice.

With a big shove from her, I fly off the platform and land on the floor. Such humiliation! Not until years later do I realize that hot chocolate is made with milk, and the shove has probably been my punishment for stupidity.

Anyhow, that day, as soon as I get home, I crawl into bed. I feel sick. Sick with shame.

Mama thinks I've come down with something, and she keeps me home the following day, which, I believe, is a Saturday. We have half days on Saturdays. By Monday, I feel better, and my awful teacher seems to have forgotten the beverage episode. I still get my hot chocolate for breakfast, which is good, because I don't like white milk. To me, the white stuff tastes slimy.

Gisela, with all her milk drinking, should have strong bones. But when she's supposed to carry something, she always complains, "It's too heavy. My arms are too tired." Indeed, she has a weakness in her arms, and the doctor also detects a slight curvature of the spine. For a while, Mama has to take her to a special clinic for exercises.

My sister also has to take a vitamin and mineral supplement called *Biomalz*. The malt looks and tastes somewhat like molasses. A long list of ingredients is printed on the label of the can, which I'm able to read but have no idea what it all means, except for vitamin-rich and iron. The names, though some of them complicated, sound nice. I put them to a melody. Gisela eventually memorizes the whole thing, too, and then we make it our daily song.

*

We have fun during the spring of 1939. Or, maybe, I simply remember more of it, because I'm already seven years old by then.

Papa takes us all to the movies, which is a new, delightful experience. First comes the showing of a newsreel. It is not the actual news content that makes the big impression on me, but the ability to view real action on the big screen. This is so much better than looking at photos taken by Mama or Papa with their camera. Here people walk and talk, cars and airplanes move, and everything is enhanced by sound effects.

The main feature is enchanting. I simply adore the cute, curly-topped Shirley Temple, who can sing and dance and knows how to manipulate the butler and the stern owners of the fancy mansion she happens to come to live in. I'm glad it all ends on a happy note.

Gisela suddenly comes up with the grand idea that she wants to fly. If she has gotten an inspiration from the planes shown in the news, I don't know. Why now? She has seen airplanes in the sky before. The Schönefeld airport, just outside Berlin's city limit, is only a very short distance from our house. Schönefeld abuts Rudow. And Gisela has watched plenty of birds in flight. Even the clumsy chickens get off the ground now and then, but they never make it very far, because their wings are clipped.

Anyhow, my sister now tries to fly herself. She attempts a good running start; she leaps into the air as high as possible, which, really, isn't very high; she flaps her arms. Her endeavors prove unsuccessful.

Jumping off a bench or a table is no good, either.

Finally, she makes herself a set of crude paper wings, and my mother has to pin them on her dress. Oh, poor, little Gisela! As hard as she tries, she can't get up into the air and flutter about. Her experiments go on for days, possibly even weeks, and then she gives up.

One beautiful Sunday morning, perhaps it is Pentecost, Papa, Mama, Gisela and I embark on an outing to Grünau, located outside our southern end of the city. We take public transportation to a certain point, then cut through the woods and arrive at a lake.

By the water's edge is a restaurant, surrounded by a big terrace. Since the weather is absolutely gorgeous, we don't want to waste a single minute of it by being indoors, and so we select a table on the

68

terrace, with a good view of the lake. Papa, after a brief consultation with Mama, gives the waiter our order. Eating out is a rarity for us and, therefore, quite exciting.

The meal is so very delicious that I will never forget it. Breaded pork tenders with fresh asparagus and potatoes! Gisela and I are allowed to sip *Maiwein*, a refreshing beverage, served in a chalice-like glass. *Maiwein*, as the name indicates, is a drink for the month of May, to salute the spring season, with tender leaves of sweet woodruff used to give the light wine its green color and delicate flavor.   For dessert, we have ice cream. What a feast! Even Gisela eats without fussing.

Later, we walk to the edge of the water and watch the boats, and the ducks, the geese, and the swans, and we play in the green meadow – carefully, for we can't get our Sunday clothes dirty.

A holiday mood is in the air. Wherever I look, people are smiling and laughing. Even the birds seem to chirp more and sing gayer tunes than in the city. The sky … it couldn't be bluer, and the sun couldn't possibly shine brighter than on this wonderful day. Everything feels so perfectly good. Our family is together, and all is right with the world.

Eventually, and much too quickly, it is time to go home. With a bit of sadness, I cast one more look at the beautiful lake and the big meadow. Then I say farewell to the terrace, where guests take their meals under colorful umbrellas.

"Let's go," Mama calls to me, and I run to take her hand. A few minutes later, Gisela and I skip along the path that goes through the woods. Along the way, we pick wildflowers and give them to Mama and Papa as presents.

After a while, we come to a crossroads. Papa wants to go one way, Mama the other. Of course, my sister and I have no idea where we are, and so we don't enter into the discussion. My mother insists her way is the correct one. My father, according to her, has no sense of direction. And here it should be mentioned that I have inherited this trait from him. Anyhow, Mama wins. Indeed, she has chosen the correct path, and we arrive safely at the clearing near the train stop.

*

My mother's friend, the one with the obnoxious son, always goes on a summer vacation to Wollin, an island in the Baltic Sea, off the Pomeranian coast. She raves about the place.

 Mama is familiar with the Baltic, for she has spent time there as a young woman, in some kind of recreation camp. The salty breezes of the Baltic are said to be beneficial to people with respiratory problems, and the mixture of needle and deciduous trees in the forests makes for easy breathing.

We have never been on a real vacation, but we're going this year. It will be just Mama, Gisela and I. Papa, unfortunately, has to stay behind, for he cannot leave his business. Actually, I wouldn't mind remaining at home for the summer, either. The thought of leaving my familiar surroundings for several weeks … such an eternity … makes me sad. Gisela, on the other hand, is raring to go. She can hardly wait to get on the train, and arrangements haven't even been made yet.

*

School lets out for the summer. Already weeks earlier, Mama has received a letter from Neuendorf on Wollin, informing her that a room will be waiting for us. The owner will be picking us up from the Warnow train station. Now it's all set. No getting away from it. I approach the situation with a mixture of excitement and misgiving. Oh, I'm such a homebody! And I hate to say good-bye to Papa … even to Muselchen, the cat. Mäuschen, our little pooch, isn't around anymore, and I can't remember when and how she has left us.

My father accompanies us to the long-distance train, which we have to board in the city. The black locomotive, pulling many cars, comes roaring into the station and stops. Gisela and I, after having hugged Papa just one more time, scramble up the high, iron steps onto the platform of the railroad car. Mama follows, and Papa hands the luggage to her. We find an empty compartment, stash our suitcases and smaller bags, and then stick our heads out the open window to exchange a few more words with my father.

"Have a wonderful vacation. Have fun. See you in a few weeks." Papa gives us a big smile. I think he's genuinely happy for us.

I'm so glad that this man standing there is my father. He's the nicest, kindest man I've ever known. He looks so tall and handsome, and his dark hair has curls just like Gisela's, only hers are blond. And her hair is longer, of course, because she's a girl, and she usually wears a big bow right on top of her head. She loves big bows.

Anyhow, our Papa stands on that platform so alone, and it just doesn't seem right that we have to leave him behind.

The stationmaster gives the signal. Our train manages a little jerk. It begins to move. My father, walking alongside the train for a short distance, reaches up to our fingertips and touches them for one more good-bye. We wave, he waves, and soon he's out of sight. My mother wipes a few tears from her eyes.

"About three hours to Stettin," she says. "Then we have to change trains."

*

It appears as if there's not much more to the landscape beyond the city limits of Berlin than endless, flat fields with cows and sheep and some horses, and stretches of forests. Not many houses are built near the railroad tracks. If towns of decent size are around, they must be off to the sides, hidden behind woods. But when we near Stettin, I know that a bustling city is coming up. Suddenly, houses appear, and streets, and many, many fancy churches, and factories, and vehicles. People! Life!

Soon we have to get off the train. So the luggage gets pulled down from the rack on top, and we carry it close to the door. We are ready, but it takes many more minutes before we reach the station.

Eventually, the train comes to an abrupt stop. We can hardly hold our balance.

"Careful with those steps," Mama warns.

Why are they so high and dangerous?

My mother struggles with the big suitcases. We kids take the small stuff. Gisela complains that her bag is too heavy.

Without trouble, we find our connecting train, and when it starts rolling, we don't have to hang our heads and arms out the window, because there's nobody to wave to this time.

We are amazed how big Stettin is. It seems as if the city doesn't want to end.

"Look over there!" My mother suddenly points to the view on the other side of the train. "This water over there is an arm of the Stettin Lagoon. We're getting close to the Baltic."

But the water is visible for a short time only, and then we are passing forests again.

Mama discovers short, bushy ground cover, and this gets her all excited. "Must be blueberries," she says.

I like the profusion of pretty flowers along the embankments. And the impressive patches of heather. Of course, Mama has to tell me first what I'm looking at, for I can't remember having seen heather before.

After less than two hours on that train, we cross water, the wide part of the lagoon, and after that, we are on the Wollin Island. Warnow, our end station, is reached soon. We are in town, but in a very, very small town. It doesn't look charming. Tourists wouldn't want to stay there.

We've barely gotten off the train, and Mama has inspected the luggage to make sure every piece is accounted for, when a slight, middle-aged man steps up to us and inquires, if we are the Beetz family.

"Yes, we are," answers my mother.

"Glad to meet you," he says. "Welcome. I'm Ernst Teetzen, and I'm here to pick you up. Marie, my wife, has your room ready. Come, follow me, my wagon is parked over there." He points to the horse and buggy waiting just a few paces away. Then he takes the suitcases from my mother and carries them for her, like a true gentleman.

I like Herr Teetzen, even though he doesn't pay much attention to Gisela and me. He's not very talkative, anyhow, but when he opens his mouth, his voice sounds nice, and he looks pleasant enough.

Soon, we are all seated up on the wagon; Herr Teetzen takes the reins and tells his horses to go. We're on the last stretch of our journey. When we travel over cobblestones, the ride goes bump, bumpy, bump, and as soon as we come to the paved road, everything is nice and smooth. Clip, clop, clip, clop go the hooves of the pretty, brown horse, and that's better than the endless chugging of the train.

At first, we pass stretches of woodland, meadows, and crop-covered fields, but when we come to the big lake that lies to our right, Herr Teetzen explains, "This is Lake Neuendorf. We're almost there."

Moments later, we turn into a dirt road and continue to just before the next corner, which also happens to be the last. Beyond that, it's only fields again and then woods. The horse knows the entrance to its home and stops in front of a row of stables. Herr Teetzen jumps off the wagon and then lends us a hand to climb down. He carries our luggage to the small building, the one he calls "summer house," which sits apart from the big main house, and we follow him.

*

We inspect our accommodations. Though a bit cramped, the bedroom is cheery enough and will do just fine. It is furnished with three beds, and Mama chooses the one by the door for herself. A washstand with a porcelain basin and a matching pitcher, both decorated with pretty flowers, and a really nice mirror above, on the wall, is toward the back of the room. We also have a closet and one or two chairs over there.

What really delights us is the fact that we have the use of a good-sized, closed-in verandah with a big table and more than enough chairs. From that verandah, we can see all the beautiful flowers in Teetzen's garden and the meadow across the road.

In the room next to ours, but not connected to the verandah, are a teacher from Stettin, his wife, and their grandson. The boy, my age, is, in my opinion, on the weird side. I have to get into this a bit later. He probably takes after his grandfather, who also appears slightly strange to me.

Our landlady, Marie, is a short, round-faced, jolly individual. She likes to talk. A few days after our arrival, she says to my mother, "Frau Beetz, I almost sent you a rejection when you inquired about a room. I was really tempted to tell you we were all filled up. Honestly, I was afraid your daughters would be like the boy of the friend who recommended us to you. But your girls are well behaved. They are a true pleasure. And you are, too. I'm glad you're here."

When I hear this, I say to myself, "Ha, ha, ha! Somebody besides me doesn't like that boy." I've never asked my sister, if she cares for his company. Of course, neither one of us would dare to tell a grownup what we think of him. That would be impolite. Children are not supposed to voice their opinion – unless asked by their parents.

*

Our vacation turns out much more delightful than I've expected. After a short while, I don't even pine for Rudow anymore. But I still miss Papa.

Every morning, we get up early and enjoy the breakfast brought to us by Marie Teetzen. She serves us rolls or bread with butter and delicious preserves. Sometimes, we get a boiled egg, too. There's always milk for Gisela and me, and coffee for Mama. With the early morning sun visiting us through the open windows, breakfast taken on the verandah tastes so very, very good. What a lovely start to a wonderful day!

It doesn't take long to straighten up our room, and then we're off to the beach. With bathing suits, towels, a comb, and some money in her bag, my mother leads the way. Gisela and I carry our own equipment: brand-new buckets with pretty pictures on the outside, and a shovel for digging in the sand.

First, we have to go through the village. After we've crossed the main road, the street curves to the left to form a semicircle. Half way around, we come to a fairly wide path, on the right, which leads to the beach. Now we walk through the forest for about twenty minutes, and it's a pleasant walk, for the woods are still and fragrant. When I look deeper into them, especially where the pines are clustered, they appear enchanted. With a bit of imagination, and I have plenty of it, I can easily visualize tiny fairies flitting around, their wings glittering in the sunbeams

77

that penetrate the dark tree canopy like golden shafts. A multitude of birds join in melodious morning song. Some call to each other, and their acknowledgements go back and forth. Gisela and I try to imitate one bird's particularly interesting sounds, and when he answers – at least we believe his trills are meant for us, we are delighted. Off and on, a little frog hops across the way. He has to be followed. And when we discover ripe blueberries a bit off the path, we stop to pick them and shove them right into our mouth. Of course, it takes a little longer than those estimated twenty minutes when we get off the track, but foraging for food, exploring nature, and even racing up and down small embankments are well worth the delay.

Suddenly, the woods end. Before us, beyond a narrow clearing, are the dunes, the beach, and the sea.

First, we have to pass Biek's Restaurant. It sits to our right. In the back room, tables are set for diners. In the front, the owners sell refreshing drinks, ice cream, candy, and postcards. Beach toys and other small items a summer guest may have forgotten to bring from home can also be bought in this place. And the Bieks rent out big, canopied beach chairs, made of wicker. The beach chairs' awnings can be let down for shade and privacy. Under the seat, the chairs have a storage chest. If people padlock this chest, they can keep their belongings in there overnight. That saves them from toting all their stuff back to their lodgings. When one of Biek's workers carries such beach chair on his back, he resembles a giant turtle out for a stroll.

After passing the restaurant, we have to go down a flight of wooden steps that lead to the beach. At about the halfway point, a small platform has been built, big enough for a tiny booth from which a vendor sells more cards and all kinds of little trinkets, and for about a dozen people to stand in front of the kiosk window or squeeze by to continue their descent. Walking across the dunes is not recommended.

Right next to that little booth is a very, very important board, nailed to a pole. On that board are posted the water and air temperatures. Believe me, those figures are rarely high. But what we have here is not hot Rudow with our little tub in the yard. This is the Baltic! It is big and beautiful. Awe-inspiring.

We pause to watch the waves. They are not fierce ones. They come rolling in. They crest. They break. White froth bubbles toward the shore. It's fascinating for a kid who has never seen the sea before.

To the left, in the distance, somewhat veiled by fog, land stretches out into the sea. "This is Usedom, Wollin's twin island," explains my mother.

"And now let's find a nice spot on the beach. It will be ours for the whole vacation," she continues. "But take your shoes off first. Here you have to walk barefooted."

With shoes in hand, we stomp through the warm,

soft sand that looks like pale, finely ground pepper. It is very clean.

We agree on a location closer to the dunes than to the water, not too terribly far from the steps. And not too far away from the plank walk that leads up to the outhouse, which, we soon find out, we rather not use, because it stinks too much. Thank God, the stench remains up there, and we cannot notice it down by the beach. We only get the fresh, salty air from the sea.

The water beckons. We can't get into our bathing suits quickly enough. It's super easy for little kids. They simply shed their play clothes and then climb into their suits. Or they frolic in the nude. Women are expert change artists. Skirts and towels provide privacy. Those articles can be used like tents, and they hide everything that shouldn't be seen. How men manage, I don't know. Perhaps, they always wear their bathing trunks under their trousers. Or they rent one of those beach chairs and let the awning down. If, however, they should show their naked butt for a minute or two, nobody would get upset and call the police.

In no time at all, we reach the edge of the water, where the sand is wet and cool. When we venture just a bit farther, the sea, with each incoming wave, laps at our feet, and Gisela and I screech, because it is unexpectedly cold. A few steps more, and the water swirls around our ankles. Here comes a wave again, and we jump, but our bottoms get wet, anyhow. We get splashed harder … we lose our balance … we are soaked from head to toe … and the water doesn't seem so chilly anymore. Yippee! The Baltic is more fun than our tub at home.

*

After our initiation to the wonderful sea, it's time to go to work. In order to establish residency on the beach, we have to build a fort, a big one, one large enough for all three of us and for our towels and other stuff to comfortably fit in. My mother makes an outline, and then the digging by hand, shovel, and bucket begins. That's some job! In the beginning, it looks as if it might take at least a week until our project will be finished. But we're good sand movers, and within two days, our circular fort wall has reached standard height when compared with others in our neighborhood. All that's left to do now is to decorate our beachfront property. It is my mother's idea to tightly pack our buckets with damp sand and then turn them over to let the sand mounds, each one looking like a Turk's hat, rest on top of our castle wall. Even though those decorative hats get spaced far enough apart, we have to form a lot of them. And each time we walk through the woods, we pick up pinecones, for they are needed to spell out our names on the outside of the castle. This way, nobody can make the mistake and accidentally move into our beach home. I believe only Gisela's and my names appear on the sand wall. But that's good enough.

81

*

For lunch, which is our main meal, we always return to the village. We have reservations at Schössow's. Many other summer visitors frequent the *Kurhaus,* meaning Spa House, which is said to be more elegant, also more expensive, and more out of the way for us. Schössow's has been recommended to us for its home style cooking and friendly atmosphere, and also for easier-on-the-pocketbook prices.

When we come from our lodgings, instead of walking around the corner, using the road, we simply go up the hill, through Teetzens' vegetable garden, past their cherry trees, and then through the always-open gate in the somewhat neglected, old wire fence. That's where Schössow's property begins. First, we cross a small, unused meadow, and then we come to a typical farmyard with ruts in the ground, made by wagon wheels and big farm equipment. In certain places, we have to watch out for chicken and goose droppings.

We pass the big barn and an open shed, where implements, wagons and carriages are kept, and where, on the side of it, a big dog is tied up. Oh, how fierce that dog appears! He barks and barks, and he pulls on his chain as if he is all set to break it and come after us.

"He probably wants attention," says my mother. Then she talks to him in a friendly, yet matter-of-fact way, from a safe distance, until he calms down. But I think she wouldn't want to meet him, if he were loose. I know I wouldn't.

After having safely gone by that dog, we're only a minute or so from the building that houses Schössow's Restaurant. A tiny post office is there, too. It occupies the corner, and its door is right next to the restaurant's entrance. Mama finds the location of that office very convenient, because she can drop her letters addressed to Papa off before we eat, and the pretty picture postcards for Oma and Opa, which she has bought at Biek's beachfront place.

When we don't need the post office first, we go right through the restaurant door, walk past the kitchen, sniff to determine what today's menu might be, and then we continue down the short hallway to the double door to the dining hall. Upon entering, we greet the already-present diners with smiles and nods, to the right and to the left, and we say, "*Mahlzeit*." This is the customary German greeting, wishing others an enjoyable time during their meal. And when we have chosen seats at one of the long tables, we repeat the same ritual to acknowledge our immediate dining companions.

They return our greetings and then also wish us a good appetite, "*Guten Appetit*," as soon as our meal is put before us. We say, "*Danke gleichfalls*," meaning, "The same to you." German folks, as a rule, are polite.

Gisela often fusses. "I'm not hungry," she declares.

"You have to eat something," my mother insists.

"My stomach hurts," Gisela whines.

Why Gisela doesn't want to eat Schössow's delicious food is beyond me. To me, this is a highly pleasant adventure. Here, on most days, we get potatoes, boiled, mashed, or made into dumplings, with meat and gravy and vegetables, all served separately. And dessert - after every meal! At home, my mother feeds us hearty soups most of the time. Meat, potatoes, and vegetables in one pot, *Eintopf*. Rice, noodles, or barley sometimes take the place of potatoes. Each food item individually heaped on the plate is for Sundays or other special occasions.

Obviously sick of my sister's constant refusal to eat, my mother resorts to a psychological trick. Now, on the way up to the restaurant, she asks, "Gisela, does your stomach hurt?"

"No."

"In that case, you can eat your food today."

It works.

On Fridays, fish, fresh from the waters of the Baltic, is being served. My mother raves about how wonderful it is, but I could do without the many fish bones. Especially, when it happens to be flounder, which has that whole row of real tiny bones around the edges. Gisela needs her fish filleted, before she even takes her first bite.

Saturdays are best. That's when we receive our absolutely favorite treat for dessert. It is blueberry cobbler, freshly baked in Schössow's kitchen. Everybody gets a thick, juicy, mouth staining, big hunk of it. Yum, yum, is this ever delicious! It is even better than Sunday's rich, creamy vanilla ice cream.

Quite often, after having eaten our scrumptious meals, we saunter, walk, or run, according to urgency, down the hill, holding our full bellies, to unload the now somewhat burdensome excess into the deep hole of the outhouse, located between Teetzens' chicken coop and the sheep barn. Thank goodness, the outhouse has two stalls, one for big folks, and the other for people with short legs. It's a very sturdy outhouse of brick construction, and it has full doors, each with a baseball-size hole toward the top and a not-too-tight fit at the bottom, for good ventilation, I guess. Though there's plenty of reading material (used for toilet paper, mainly) lying around, none of the occupants of this facility seem to overdo their stay. This is fortunate, because of the number of people who have to use the outhouse.

Marie Teetzen, well aware of our using the shortcut to Schössow's, warns us, "Be careful. Watch out for the geese. They can be vicious. When they don't want you to cross their yard, they may try to attack you. Pretend you don't see them. Calmly walk away. Don't look back. Don't attempt to chase them."

We are confident that no silly geese will harm us. They're probably already used to us just like that not-so-loud-anymore yapping dog. But one day, out of the blue, as we are walking toward Teetzens' gate, the huge gander races around Schössow's barn, his long neck outstretched, wings flapping, and he gives off the most threatening goose-war cry I've ever heard.

"Walk fast, but don't run," my mother tells us. She stays behind Gisela and me, like a shield, to protect us from the enemy.

Suddenly, I hear a thud. Then a scream from Mama.

Ignoring the order to keep on walking, I stop. I turn around. I see that the gander has attacked my mother. With his beak, he tears at the hem of her flowery dress. He thrashes his enormous wings like a maniac. Oh, it is a frightening sight.

My poor mother! She swings her purse and hits the wild, feathered beast with all her might, again and again, until he finally lets go and retreats.

Mama lets out a sigh of relief. Then she pretends nothing that terribly bad has happened, and we keep on using the shortcut for the rest of our Neuendorf vacation. The geese never bother us again.

*

In the afternoon, we usually waste little time to return to the beach. Why use precious moments for naps like our vacation neighbors from Stettin? They come strolling down hours after us. Sometimes they put their blankets and other stuff near our sand fort, and then we can watch them. It's a sight to behold! The grandfather goes to test the water. First, he gets his toes wet … very carefully. Then he ventures into the water up to his ankles, perhaps. He seems to contemplate, if he should get wet a bit more or stay dry. Okay, he decides to be courageous. He bends down, scoops up some cold water and splashes it over his thick arms and fat belly. Having that much accomplished, he turns and strides back to his wife and grandson.

"Time to go for a swim," he tells the skinny boy.

"But, but … the water is too cold," whines the kid. "I don't like the ocean."

"The Baltic is not an ocean. It is a sea," corrects the grandfather, using his stern teacher face.

"Come on now, darling," coaxes the grandmother, who, by the way, never goes near the water herself. "Give it a try, please."

"No! No! Leave me be!"

"Look here, boy, we didn't bring you to the Baltic for nothing. And a bit of water won't hurt you." The grandfather seems to lose his temper, and I can hardly wait to find out what will happen next.

"I'll give you a twenty-five pfennig piece, if you go in." The grandmother digs out her wallet and produces a shiny coin.

It works. Though not looking very happy, the funny boy lets his grandfather take his hand and lead him to the edge of the water. Eventually, after a lot of screeching and trying to escape the splashing waves, he does get wet and is forced to endure the hated element.

Gisela and I, and Mama immediately behind us,

race to see who can make it first into the water, and we pass right by the funny pair to let them see how much fun we're having.

The boy is an absolute wimp. My opinion of him is reinforced, when, one evening, as I'm sitting on our verandah steps, he challenges me to a shoving contest.

"I can push you from the starting line all the way over to the gate," he boasts.

"We'll see," I say.

He draws a line in the sand. We take our positions, put our hands together, and then we push. Seconds later, howling, he's on his way, backward, in the direction of the verandah.

"Not fair," he protests. "I didn't have a solid footing."

"Try again," I say.

And so it goes on and on, until we're both tired of this silly contest.

Sometimes, in the evenings, the summer guests congregate in the meadow across the dirt road. The grownups chat; the children amuse themselves playing ball, jumping rope, or just horsing around.

One evening, a cute boy with a mop of blond curls comes by to join us. His name is Siegbert, and he's a local. I have a feeling he wants to show off in front of us, and he does all kinds of tricks, rather expertly. He knows how to do somersaults, cartwheels, handstands, and he amazes us with a headstand.

But, oh my goodness, his head comes down in a rather bad spot. In the center of a nice, fat cow plop!

For a moment, his face shows bewilderment. Then it changes to disgust. Without saying good-bye, he runs home. A few people laugh. I feel sorry for him.

Bello, the tan dog from next door, comes running. The little male mutt heads straight for the teacher from Stettin, lifts his hind leg, and generously sprinkles him with the yellow contents of his bladder. The man, his shirt all wet, jumps up and is outraged. A new volley of laughter erupts. I join in. I believe Bello has wanted to show his dislike of a certain summer guest and make this payback time.

*

When the weather is on the dreary side, we go into the woods and pick blueberries. They are the small, wild ones, and extremely tasty. It's fun to gather berries. It's even more fun to eat them by the handful or from a bowl, with milk and sugar. Off and on, we have a companion, who likes to come with us into the woods. This is Purzel, our landlady's small, shaggy, black and white female mutt, whose son, brave Bello, has revenged Siegbert after people have made fun of the boy's misfortune.

Purzel loves blueberries. She begs for them. In the beginning, we feed her, and we think it's funny the way she dances in front of us and opens her mouth until one of us plops a blue goodie into it. Eventually, we get fed up with her antics, and then my mother tells her off.

"Purzel, down there! You get your own," she

orders and points to the short, stubby plants.

What a smart dog! She actually knows how to pick blueberries with her own little mouth.

"Of course she knows how," Marie Teetzen says when my mother tells her about it. "Do you perhaps think that I would pick berries for her, when we go into the woods together?"

Frau Teetzen takes advantage of the blueberry season, and she brings home big buckets full of the delicious fruit. What she doesn't use up right away, she preserves for the winter. It would be nice, if we could take some berries home to Berlin, at least a few for Papa to taste.

"They would go bad," Mama says.

*

I cannot recall how long we are staying in Neuendorf that year. It may have been for four glorious weeks. But I do remember that the time went by with lightning speed.

Gisela cries when we walk to the beach one last time to say farewell to the Baltic. I'm a bit sad, too. The idea of going home, to the place I love, and, especially, to see Papa again, makes the impending departure much easier to bear.

Before Herr Teetzen loads our luggage into the wagon, his wife comes out of the house to wish us a safe trip home. She shakes our hands and says, "We hope to see you again next year."

"We will come back, for sure," answers my mother.

"We will," chimes in my little sister.

And then we're off to the train station in Warnow. From there it's only about four hours to Berlin, where Papa will be waiting for us. Yes, I'm looking forward to that.

*

Something is in the wind. I hear snatches of what my parents are discussing.

"They say we're not supposed to buy from the Jews anymore, but they're my best suppliers." Papa looks worried. I rarely ever see him this way.

"You already mentioned this last year. You said you had to be careful." Mama's voice betrays her alarm.

"I am."

"What are you going to do, Kurt?"

"I really don't know. I've been dealing with them for so many years. Just drop them? That doesn't seem fair. They are good people, and they have to make a living, too."

"Then be extra careful."

I have no idea what's going on, and I soon forget about it. School starts again, we are back to the old routine, and life is the way it's supposed to be, as far as I'm concerned.

In the fall, a traveling circus comes to Rudow. The big tent goes up where the amusement park has been before. Since not much ever happens in our area, it is a big deal to see a circus show.

I do remember my very first impression. Upon entering the tent, I notice that it smells heavily of animals. In my opinion, it stinks.

The clowns amuse me. They act really stupid. Their antics make me laugh.

A pretty girl in a fancy costume does marvelous tricks on a good-looking horse. I admire her.

Elephants are being herded in, and they have to perform dance steps. How can big, clumsy pachyderms learn to move to music and remember a routine? That's amazing!

When it's time for the tiger act, I would rather not be there. This looks dangerous. Tigers should be in the zoo, in big cages.

And when the trapeze artists and the tightrope walker perform their stunts, I cringe. No, no, this is asking for trouble! What if one of them falls? They should have a safety net or a bouncy cushion. If it were up to me, I would make it a law. Many, many years later, in my old age, I still feel the same. I also have to admit that I've never been to a live circus performance since that day in 1939.

CHAPTER THREE

THE WAR YEARS

A dark cloud settles over our once so carefree days. The radio is not always tuned to the music station, and my mother doesn't sing as often as has been her habit. The newscast is on more frequently. My mother looks worried. When my father comes home from work at night, the conversation turns serious.

"The last war started when I was seven," I hear my mother say. "Now Eva is seven, and here it comes again. Why does it have to happen?"

"Maybe it will be over quickly," my father tries to comfort her.

"I don't know. I have such a terrible feeling."

"War is always bad. Ordinary people don't want to fight. I certainly don't want to be a soldier. I don't want to be forced to shoot another human being."

I have no idea what war is like, but I assume it is something horrible. And to think of Papa having to shoot somebody, that's absolutely unimaginable.

Then it happens. A letter arrives in the mail. It's an official one, addressed to Kurt Beetz. My mother has a panic attack. She cries. When my father opens it, his eyes fill with sadness; he looks as if he holds in his hands the news about somebody's death.

"I'm drafted," he says.

"No!" screams my mother. "You can't go!"

93

"I'll have to obey orders."

For a while, they cling to each other, and I'm pretty sure they're both crying.

Eventually, Papa explains the situation to Gisela and me, and we are very sad. But he assures us he'll not be gone very long. The war will be over soon. Then we can all be together again and build the new house on Fleischerstraβe. All will be well. Of course, if Papa says so, it has to be true. I trust him.

Soon, Papa is gone. Onkel Willi has to leave, too, and so does Onkel Martin. It doesn't seem fair.

*

Tante Uschi comes to live with us for a while. She takes care of Gisela and me while my mother tends to the business until it is liquidated. My aunt sleeps in Papa's bed.

One night, strange noises come from behind our house. Footsteps. I believe my mother has heard them first. She turns on the light, sneaks to the window and peeks out from behind the curtain. Tante Uschi sits up in bed and begins to laugh, really loud. It isn't that she considers the matter funny. No. That's the way she always reacts when she's scared. Anyhow, my mother reports that she sees a man jump over the fence and then take off across the neighbor's yard.

"Thank you for that outburst of laughter," she says to my aunt. "This man probably thought we had a party going on with all kinds of people present. So,

94

instead of breaking in, he ran away."

It is nice that Tante Uschi keeps us company. She is young and pretty, and she has such a pleasant giggle. But as soon as my mother is done with the store business and able to stay home again, my aunt returns to her own apartment.

Oma visits us once a week, usually on Wednesdays. Since she likes puddings for lunch, it becomes a tradition that my mother cooks vanilla pudding, also a gelatin dessert, which we call *Glibberpudding*, because it jiggles, and red *Götterspeise,* food for the gods, which is tapioca cooked in fruit juice. We also have chocolate soup, real dark and bitter, for this is the way Oma enjoys it. My sister and I would prefer milk and sugar in that chocolate soup, but what can we do? Oma is our guest, and we don't dare to grumble. Of course, when my grandmother isn't around, we don't eat puddings for lunch. Once a week, though, it is kind of fun.

Großer Opa comes off and on to check up on us. When something needs to be done, which is too hard to handle for my mother, like cleaning out the cesspool, for instance, or killing a chicken, he gladly lends a hand. He is really good to us.

Letters from my father arrive almost daily. Once in a while, he's allowed to come home for a weekend. It's like a holiday then. But since we never know in advance, when he's going to show up, Mama, at times, is a bit skittish about leaving the house, for she doesn't want to miss a single minute of his visit.

It's mid-morning, on a Saturday, I believe, when we're in the food section of Karstadt, the big department store in Neukölln, and she suddenly announces, "We have to buy meat and then hurry home. I have a feeling Papa will come today." She quickly picks out some wild boar and a few other items, pays, and then we rush to ride back to Rudow. Happiness reigns when we find Papa already in bed, his head hidden under the covers and his feet sticking out at the bottom. Mama claims she has a sixth sense.

*

Onkel Willi comes home, too, off and on. Of course, he always stops in to say hello to us. Each time he comes, he has a little present for Gisela and me. If he doesn't have a chance to buy us a trinket, he raids Tante Lotte's drawers for things he considers appropriate, like hankies or a cheap piece of jewelry. Tante Lotte gets mad at him for that, but he doesn't care. He always tells her, "You don't need all this stuff."

One day, as my mother, Gisela and I happen to be out in our garden, we hear a commotion coming from my aunt's house. It turns out, Coco, Onkel Willi's dwarf parrot, has escaped. We see the colorful bird. It flies to the tree near the garage and rests on a high branch.

Tante Lotte comes running, and she keeps calling, "Coco, come back!"

Coco, motionless, remains on his lofty perch.

My mother carefully walks to the tree. Gisela and I tiptoe closer, too. We do not want to scare the bird. Soon we all join in the pleading. But Coco, probably enjoying his freedom, just sits, cocks its head and listens.

My poor aunt wrings her hands. She cries. She cajoles.

Coco probably relishes the attention.

"Please come down," Tante Lotte whines.

The bird nods its head. But this doesn't mean it is willing to make a move.

"Coco, pretty bird, hop on my shoulder!" My aunt makes an inviting gesture.

We all try to coax the parrot down with sweet talk and beautiful promises. Nothing happens.

"What is Willi going to say when he finds out?" my aunt laments.

At that moment, Onkel Willi, in uniform, makes his unexpected appearance. Without saying a word to any of us, he goes into his house. When he comes back out, he has his small accordion slung around his neck. He begins to play. Standing under the tree, he makes eye contact with the little escapee. And if I'm not mistaken, that tiny rascal up there winks at his master, and it gives off some happy sounds which probably mean, "Am I glad to see you and hear your music again."

Coco rocks back and forth for a bit, makes himself

tall, then glides down from his high place and gently lands on Onkel Willi's shoulder. Together, the two friends return into the house. Tante Lotte follows, and I'm sure she closes the door behind her so that Coco has no chance to fly off again.

*

As winter approaches, talk abounds, like in the previous year, about the poor in the country who need help. My mother and my aunt contribute to the food drives. Somebody stops by for the weekly donations. Clothes are also wanted. People are told to conserve fuel.

Germany has an unemployed population, concentrated in certain mountainous areas, like in the Erzgebirge (Ore Mountains), for example, and times are especially bad for those folks during the winter months. But Hitler has come up with an idea to bring work to the idle. They are introduced to cottage industries and taught to manufacture tiny toys, which are then shipped to the cities to be sold by street vendors, probably volunteers. Everybody loves those cute items, and they are really inexpensive. Each week, something new is on the market – miniature wooden dolls, animals, and the tiniest fairy tale books, also Christmas ornaments, spin tops, and so much more. Gisela and I are delighted when Mama buys more for our collection.

Papa is allowed to spend a few days with us shortly before Christmas. As far as I can remember, he cannot stay for the holidays. None of the men are around, only the grandfathers. But while my father is briefly with us, he and Mama are planning something super special. We are all going to see a show, live, on stage! It's a children's performance, and it's wonderful. The story is about some bad youngsters who don't want to listen to what their parents have to say. Just like in Pinocchio, they are lured into a land where kids are allowed to do as they please. In this play, it is the land of the trolls. All day long, the naughty main characters cavort with their new friends and do things forbidden in their own homes, but when they discover hair growing on their bodies, in places where no hair is supposed to be, they are gripped with fear. No, no, they don't want to turn into trolls! They swear, from this moment on, they will be good children, as long as they will look normal again and are allowed to return home to their parents. Naturally, all ends well.

After the show, and still months later, Gisela and I keep singing snippets of what we have heard, especially the happy chorus of the trolls who proclaim that they always do as they wish, and it would be laughable, if anybody should try to change their naughty ways. We also gather handfuls of dried grasses, and we push and pull and twist them into troll shapes. Then, of course, we sing our favorite troll song over and over again.

Mama wants to be extra nice to Papa and spoil him a little while he has his few days with us. So, one evening, for supper, she fries pork chops, and she fixes two for him. Everybody has one on the plate, and the extra chop is still sitting on the table. When my father has finished his piece of meat, she tells him to help himself to the second one.

He shakes his head. "Why am I supposed to have more than you?' he asks. "It wouldn't be fair."

"Because you always like pork chops so very much, and you are here so rarely, and you probably don't get such nice food in your army kitchen, and because we love you, and we want you to have it."

Mama has stated her case. Gisela and I nod in agreement. But Papa takes a knife and cuts the meat into four pieces. Then he insists we share.

After supper, since we are in an extra special, happy mood, we turn into little show-offs. We pretend to be Max and Moritz, German storybook characters, who have just eaten their fill of roasted chicken, stolen from a neighbor. In the picture book illustration, the two bad boys are propped against a tree, their legs stretched out in front of them, their full bellies protruding, and a chicken leg is sticking out of Max's and Moritz's mouth.

Our bellies are also full. Gisela and I plop down on the floor and, with our backs against the big closet, we imitate the bad boys. But instead of a chicken leg, we each have the bone from our pork chop sticking out of the mouth. Papa joins us on the floor. Mama laughs. It is so good when the whole family is united!

*

My parents have decided to spend New Year's Eve together, in Neuruppin, a distance north of Berlin, where my father is stationed. I am allowed to go along. Gisela has to stay with Oma and Opa.

Mama and I take the train, and when we get to Neuruppin, we find the hotel room, which my father has booked for us. We have to wait until Papa is off duty, and then he picks us up for supper. I'm really glad to see him again. It is also exciting to go out to eat, because we do it so very, very seldom.

Somehow, it is hard for me to get used to seeing my father in uniform. The constant saluting also bewilders me. A friendly hello should suffice. It doesn't work in the military, I'm told.

The more the evening progresses, the greater the crowd becomes in the restaurant. And the noisier it gets. Soldiers and their wives or girlfriends eat and drink and talk and drink, and they laugh and sing and drink, and the music is quite loud. The cigarette smoke gets thick. Not even the balloons and the party hats and the festive streamers put me in the mood for celebrating. I've never been up for a New Year's Eve celebration before. I'm not used to staying up this late. But when the countdown to midnight begins, I perk up and join in the shouting of "Happy New Year." I blow my noisemaker like everybody else, and I wouldn't want to miss the hugging and kissing that follows.

"How much longer will this war go on?" I hear my mother ask.

"I don't know," my father says with a deep sigh.

1940 has begun. Mama and I return to Rudow. My father remains in Neuruppin.

*

The winter drags on. I get a sore throat again, which happens quite frequently, but this time it's pretty bad. Of course, I have to stay in bed … kids always need bed rest until the illness is completely gone. And whenever I have a sore throat, I have to wear a woolen stocking around my neck. According to Oma, such stocking shouldn't be freshly laundered. A woolen one, already worn for a day or more works better. That's an oldwives tale. Mama lets me use a clean one to keep my throat warm. Or she wraps a big scarf around my neck, a few times, which is even warmer than a stocking.

As soon as my fever is down, and I feel better, but not well enough to be let out of bed, I crochet clothes for my tiniest doll. Making a dress is easy enough, but working on a miniature hat is a different story. This requires patience, for I have to start with only very few stitches before adding, off and on, an extra one, and I constantly have to measure to make sure it's just right and not too big or too small for that little doll's head. And then I try to crochet booties! They don't turn out well at all. They look like teensy blobs. I give up.

Gisela is good company while I'm sick in bed. She is always willing to play dolls with me. Perhaps, she is happy that I'm cooped up at home all day and have so much time for her.

I can't get to the dollhouse, a simple two-room affair with an open front and no roof, built by Onkel Gerhard, the carpenter, but a few pieces of the doll furniture, also crafted by my uncle, have room on my bed. Most of the action, we pretend, takes place outdoors - on the wintry slopes of my white pillow. Our doll kids are allowed to slide down to their hearts' content. After a good rest from their strenuous activities, they have to go to school. I am always the teacher. Because my sister's little ones have to be instructed together with mine and are expected to learn, Gisela, without realizing it, gets an education as well. This prepares her for first grade, which she will be entering in a few months.

*

Spring arrives. Easter follows a week later. Despite the war, the Easter bunny delivers sweets. He even brings a marzipan egg for my mother. It is not as big as in previous years, but, still, it is marzipan, her absolute favorite Easter food. And, as usual, by the time Gisela and I wake up in the morning, that marzipan egg is half eaten.

"Look here," Mama says, showing us what is left of the egg, "the Easter bunny brought me an egg that's been badly nibbled, again. It's not nice of him."

Of course, we do not believe her. We are used to her gluttony when it comes to marzipan Easter eggs.

When Onkel Martin hears about this episode, he promises Mama a ten-pound egg as soon as the war is over. He wants to make it for her, with his own hands. She never gets it.

My sister's Easter eggs disappear reasonably fast, but mine might collect dust, if other people wouldn't help themselves to them. First arrives my classmate from across the street. Somehow, she has weaseled her way over to our house. She brazenly snitches some eggs from my basket. She doesn't ask; she just takes. How rude! Mama then hides the basket.

Even without this girl coming over, the amount of eggs in my basket gets less and less. Though I don't really mind, I wonder what is going on.

"The mice come at night and eat your candy," explains my mother.

I believe her story.

But way before the first one of my eggs disappears in a mysterious way, actually just three days after Easter, on March 30, my little sister has to go to school for the first time.

"That's not fair," she protests. "It's my birthday. I can't go to school today."

"Yes, you have to go, even if it's your birthday," says my mother. "Now get ready."

"Where are my white knee socks?"

"Sorry, no white knee socks. Put on your long stockings."

"But it's my birthday. I always wear white knee socks on my birthday."

"Not this year. It's much too cold. You would

freeze your legs off."

Whining follows.

It is getting late. Finally, Gisela, holding on to my mother with one hand and clasping the colorful first-day-of-school cone under her free arm, gets on her way to the old school in town. I, the new third grader, head in the other direction, to the Wildmeisterdamm Elementary School, which houses all grades from three to eight.

*

I now have to walk in the direction of the satellite church building and then take a path that leads through green fields of young grain. If I leave half an hour before classes begin, I make it with a few minutes to spare. And, I should mention here, that I haven't been to Sunday school since first grade started, because we are being taught religion in school. It is a required subject. Hitler has not discouraged religion yet.

I do not remember much about my third grade teacher except that she loves to pick on me. When she asks a very hard question and nobody has the answer, she still expects me to come up with the correct one. If I'm stumped, she shakes her head and says, "Eva, I really thought you would know it."

Why am I supposed to be so all knowing when nobody else is? It upsets me.

I develop a little friendship with Margitta, a classmate who lives in the center of Rudow, in a very nice, big house. Her father is a dentist, I believe, and he has not been drafted like so many other men. He may be too old. My friend is so lucky.

We celebrate her birthday, and after the other guests have left, I am allowed to stay a little longer. She takes me into her bedroom, one she has all to herself, and we play with her dollhouse. This is the grandest dollhouse I've ever seen. It has many rooms, and they have doors that open and close, and windows with curtains, and fancy furniture, and lights that can be turned on and off. Imagine! And the house has a roof, which can be lifted off. Though I am impressed, I am not jealous.

During our short breaks between classes, the girls trade *Oblaten*, colorful, high-gloss pictures, embossed and real pretty, which come in sheets of nine or twelve, or even more, according to the size of those pictures. They have to be gently ripped apart at the adjoining corners before they can be exchanged … or filed away and treated as prized collector items. Sheets of pictures are sold in stationery and bookstores, and they are relatively inexpensive. What a selection to pick from! Fairytale scenes are popular, and pictures of boys and girls in fancy, old-fashioned, outfits. Golden-haired angels with chubby faces and rosy cheeks are in demand. Dogs and cats and all kinds of wild animals are well liked, and pretty butterflies, and flowers in baskets or bouquets. One set of pictures is always lovelier than the other.

The trading of *Oblaten* usually goes like this: One

large picture for two smaller ones. Or one for one, if they are the same size and both are in equally good or slightly damaged condition. Since each sheet has so many pictures of the same category, girls may want to sacrifice one of their cute dog pictures for one of a beautiful rose, for instance. And in case someone has doubles, it's easy. Getting rid of the duplicates for something else is not a bad idea.

Open trading is fair. There are no surprises. The alternate kind of trading is for those who take chances. It works this way: Take an old notebook. Fold the pages to form pockets. Put a picture in each pocket. Honest kids insert a mixture of pictures, some large ones, some small ones, and they make sure that all of them are in good shape. Along comes someone who wants to take a chance and offers a picture. If the girl with the hidden pictures in her notebook pockets likes it, she will hold out her book and let the other girl chose one of the pockets. Then comes the surprise. Sometimes, it's a good trade; other times, it's a big disappointment. Deceitful kids choose only their smallest, most worn, dog-eared pictures, the ones they are trying to get rid of, the sneaky way. They are found out eventually, and nobody wants to deal with them anymore.

*

That spring, Muselchen has kittens. I watch how they are born. When Ursula, a girl a few years my senior, who lives a bit down the street, asks me about the birthing process, I tell her, "The cat made meow three times, and then the kittens were in the basket." Ursula, apparently not satisfied with my explanation, walks away without giving me another look. But that's exactly the way it has been. Can I help it?

Whenever Mama, Gisela and I go out, Muselchen follows us to the corner where Ursula lives with her parents. When we pass by again, our cat, still there, patiently waiting for our return, gets up from her resting place between the bushes and walks home with us. What would she do, if we decided to come back a different route?

*

Since we have enjoyed our vacation stay at the Baltic so much the previous year, Mama has registered us again with the Teetzens. This time, we are staying in the big house, on the second floor. We have a bedroom and a kitchen. Actually, the kitchen is not much more than an extension of the landing on top of the staircase. It has a wood stove, which is rather hard to light, a narrow kitchen closet to hold dishes and supplies, a small, old table to prepare food on, and a bench that holds the water bucket. To get water, we go down to the big hand pump.

Since we now have cooking facilities, we do not have to go to Schössow's. Only on special occasions, we use the restaurant.

Sometimes, I am allowed to bring the sheep in

from the meadow. When they have been grazing up on the hill, I have to be very careful that they do not drag me down the embankment. The sheep seem to like me. Even the ram with the big horns comes up to me for attention. But Adalbert, the young man who lives in the downstairs room with his mother, is afraid of animals, especially of the ram. He comes along only once, out of curiosity, I think, and I hand him the long, heavy ropes that are tied around the two female sheep's necks. I take the ram. As soon as the wooly beasts begin to pull, he screams. Then he quickly hands the whole bunch over to me. I am only eight years old; Adalbert is eighteen. When the grownups find out about this, they laugh.

Adalbert is a scared pussycat when it comes to sheep, but he believes himself to be a tiger with women. Oh, how he brags about his popularity at the nightspot he has discovered. It must be the Kurhaus that has evening entertainment. Adalbert also knows about the nude beach, which is hidden in a cove, where regular bathers wouldn't suspect it. Of course, this is where he likes to go. His mother does not divulge information about her bathing habit. Perhaps, she also likes to romp in the nude but is too shy to admit it.

Not only does Adalbert brag about his prowess with woman, which is a subject that really shouldn't be discussed in front of two little girls, but he also tries to impress everybody with the fact that he's studying to be an actor, at the Arts Institute in Berlin. If he is permitted to finish his courses and perhaps lands a job as an entertainer, I have no idea. Most likely, he is called into service like all the other young men who have to fight for their country.

Since Muselchen is not allowed to be on vacation with us, and Mama apparently has not dared to ask Tante Lotte to take care of the cat during our absence, the feline has been taken to a shelter for a holiday of her own. At least, this is how my mother has described it to Gisela and me. But when we return to Rudow, we find a letter notifying us of Muselchen's sad demise. "Due to sudden illness," it states. I believe she has died of a broken heart. We are all sad. Now we have no more pets.

*

 Letters from Papa arrive on a fairly regular basis. When she finds none in the mailbox for a while, Mama worries herself sick. Ever since my father has been on the Western front and seen battle, his life has been at risk. He has moved through Belgium and the Netherlands, and now he is stationed somewhere in France. We have tons of pictures from those foreign countries, even some taken in Paris.

According to my father, the French people are very friendly to the German soldiers. They even invite them into their homes. When the soldiers see hungry Frenchmen, children and old folks especially, they feed them. Papa wonders why nations cannot get along. People are the same everywhere. A few are evil, but the majority of all mankind is decent and peace loving.

About Paris, my father reports, "The subways stink. The French don't pay much attention to their personal hygiene. They don't wash their bodies often enough, and then they douse themselves with too much perfume."

We also find out that Papa has officially been assigned the job of leading his fellow soldiers in singing. Soldiers always sing while marching, that's a known fact. This leadership duty has been given to him because of his good voice, his perfect pitch, and his knowledge of so many songs. Papa's talents have been officially discovered. We, his family, have always believed his voice to be good, even though his teacher from so very, very long ago has not been able to recognize it.

One day, a package arrives with goodies from France. Papa has included a box of chocolate candies and a note that says, "Eat the papers that hold the candies."

Is this a joke? Eat paper?

We give it a try.

Surprise! The paper is sweet. It melts in your mouth.

The next day, I take some of this miracle paper to school, and I urge a few of my best friends to eat a little piece. They laugh at me. They shake their heads. So I put a piece in my mouth and show them how it softens on my tongue. Now they are willing to give the paper a try. Ah, it really is edible! The girls are amazed.

"It's from France," I explain.

I do not take any of the chocolates to school. They are too precious to be shared.

*

Toward the end of August 1940, the radio broadcast brings bad news. Bombs have accidentally been dropped on London. The British are mad, of course. We immediately get to feel their retaliation. Under the cover of night, enemy planes fly over Berlin and drop their bombs. Now Hitler is incensed, and he issues orders to bombard London, without mercy.

We shudder. What horrors will come next?

Black shades have to cover our windows to keep the lights from shining out at night. When the enemy can't see the illumination, he doesn't know exactly where the city is. But the British pilots have a fairly good idea. When attacks are launched on industrial sites and any place thought of being important to the war effort, bombs get sprayed all over the suspected areas.

The British terrorize us with their bombs; the Germans do it to the people of Great Britain. The daily reports are horrible.

Since we have the Schönefeld airport close by, we are right in the field chosen for destruction.   The sirens wail at night. We quickly slip into our clothes, run over to Tante Lotte's house and take cover in her small basement, the place meant to store her canned goods, apples, and potatoes. The trap door gets pulled down. Then we huddle close together, jump with each loud sound of a nearby detonation, and hold our breath. When our dim, overhead light bulb flickers, we fear to be left in darkness. Only after a while, when we get accustomed to the attacks, do we think of keeping a flashlight, candles, and matches, as well as blankets in our little bomb shelter.

Gisela is awfully scared. She clings to Mama. Often, she cries. I play with my tiny, hand-held toy. It requires a steady hand to make the little steel ball, via a spiral groove, go up to the top of the mound that is under the clear dome cover. One small wiggle, and the ball rolls down again. By concentrating on the game, I do not have to think about the danger. I try to block out the hum of the aircraft, as they pass right overhead; I do not want to pay attention to the swishing sounds of the bombs that fall from the sky. I only give a little shudder when the bursting of bombs, too close for comfort, makes an earsplitting noise and shakes the ground.

One night, when the attack goes on too long, Tante Lotte feels the fullness of her bladder. She cannot hold it any longer and, during a lull in the commotion from enemy planes and explosions, she dares to climb out of the cellar to heed nature's call. Suddenly … a terrible bang! A huge tremor! It feels as if the whole house is going to come crushing down. Tante Lotte literarily flies back down into the shelter and speedily pulls the door shut. Her trembling doesn't stop for a long time.

When the all-clear signal is given, and we gingerly open the trap door to peek out to see if the house is still standing, we are happy to find only a window broken. Shattered glass is easier to take than a roof or even a whole building gone.

Our own house is still standing, too, and we are grateful for having been spared one more time.

A beautiful residence, just a bit down the road, has been hit and totally demolished. From this, we obviously have felt the big tremor.

When bombings occur before midnight, school begins at the regular time. Is the all clear signal given after midnight, classes are delayed. Nonetheless, we are often bleary-eyed in the morning. Sometimes, we would rather sleep than listen to our teacher.

The government needs money to manufacture tanks, weapons and ammunition. The war costs a lot of money.

"Sacrifice your gold, your silver. Women, give us your wedding rings," they say.

Mama will never part with her little wedding band. It means too much to her. Also, she is not patriotic. Nobody in our immediate or extended family is.

"Conserve fuel!" Pictures of an ugly, dark, male character with a sack on his shoulder are plastered everywhere. This is *Kohlenklau*, the coal thief, waster of precious energy. His mean visage greets us from every billboard, from every bridge support, from every trolley car.

Of course, we have ration cards. Many food items are in short supply, but we do not go hungry. Mama still bakes cakes, and they still taste delicious, even though she has to skimp on certain ingredients or leave them out altogether.

Onkel Willi is stationed somewhere in the East. He is the most unwilling soldier, and the family fears he may be careless and openly voice his opposition to Hitler and the war, which would get him into the deepest trouble. What trouble? Nobody has told me yet that dissenters get shot.

When Onkel Gerhard has to report for duty, I don't remember. But he gets in with the medics, which makes it less dangerous for him.

*

One day, during heating season, my mother and I go out to the shed to get some coal for the stove. My mother ducks in and makes her way to the back. I have to wait outside, for is very cramped in that shed. It is also not the cleanest place, and I shouldn't get dirty.

Mama has barely disappeared into the shed, when I hear her say, "I wonder why Kurt threw that brush in the corner. It doesn't belong there."

Then follows a scream. Mama bursts out of the shed. The brush, which really isn't a brush but a hedgehog, is stuck to her hand. By the time she gets rid of the animal, which must've been holding his winter nap by the stacked coals or the woodpile, it is minus a few of its quills. Those needle-like things have to be carefully removed from my mother's hand. She suffers considerable pain from all those pricks.

Gisela and I, after having finished our homework, now play indoors a lot, for it is mighty cold outside. Our dollhouse gets put up almost daily, and the tiny doll kids are always going to school and have to learn new stuff. We very much regret that there's no dad in our little family. Since we don't want to pretend he's a soldier, far away from home, we say he's on a business trip or on vacation.

The stores don't sell male dolls the size of our mama doll, and so, out of necessity, my mother sews one for us. Now we can let the dad come home from work and enjoy the evenings with his wife and children. We all agree the new doll looks very much like Herr Dohnt, our round-faced neighbor.

When a beautiful blanket of snow covers the ground, Gisela and I are allowed to go sledding. About ten minutes away from our house, not too far from the satellite church, is a sandpit, which, when covered with snow, is the ideal winter sport spot for all the neighborhood kids. Our hills, the sides of the pit, are pretty steep. Since the sand haulers are not very particular with the way they excavate the sand, they leave ugly rough spots. Mounds and humongous holes can easily cause a youngster to fall off his sled. My sister and I try to stay away from those danger areas. Still, after each start, we hold our breath and feel our spine tingle during the fast ride down. Then, when we've safely reached the bottom of the pit, we give a sigh of relief, get ourselves up, and are ready to drag the sled to the top again, so the thrill ride can be repeated. Hold on tight; whoosh, down it goes!

Gisela likes to ride double with me. I always sit in front and steer, and she is in the back, her arms tightly wrapped around my waist.

If it gets too crowded on the slopes, extra care is in order, for it can happen that two sleds collide, and then somebody may get hurt. Most kids are courteous, but, occasionally, a few unruly boys appear, and they are out to terrorize the girls. In that case, Gisela and I clear out as fast as we can. We do not want to get rammed and knocked off our sled.

Only when we're on our way home, do we notice the effects of the cold. Red noses, icy cheeks, tingling fingers, and feet that are almost numb. It's a good thing that we only have to walk for about ten minutes, and then, with Mama's help, can shed our snow-caked outer garments. Oh, does it feel good to be in the house again, and to warm up by the stove while sipping a cup of hot chocolate!

*

The winter passes. Air raids are the norm. People seem to have accepted them as a dangerous

117

nuisance. They only talk about them after a very close hit in the neighborhood or when someone related or befriended has been bombed out.

On rare occasions, we go to see a movie in town. What we are shown in the newsreels is not pretty. Fighting at the front, destruction, troops marching, much flag waving. The *Fuehrer* makes a speech. Yes, The Germans are going to win this war. It's a certainty. "*Sieg Heil, Sieg Heil*," shouts the crowd.

We are impatiently waiting for the promised peace. We want our father to return home. We want to be a whole family again.

*

Spring has arrived. The air is already balmy, but Gisela and I still have to wear our warm dresses. Mama even sends us out with our jackets on. Worse yet, we are still in long stockings, which are held up by the hated, long, elastic, suspender-like straps, dangling from a *Leibchen,* an undergarment like a buttoned-in-the-back vest, made of flannel material. Thank goodness, we are freed of the itchy union suit with an opening in the back for emergencies. This suit is a must during the frigid winter months.

"All the other girls are allowed to wear knee socks," laments my sister. "They are so lucky."

I wholeheartedly agree.

"Why do we have to sweat with these stockings on?" she continues.

"I know it doesn't seem fair," I say. "But Mama

always thinks we'll get sick, if we aren't dressed warm enough."

Together, we sigh, moan, grumble, and moan some more, and our steps slow to a weary trudge. Honestly, our mother can be so unreasonable, so unfair, so very uncaring. At least, that's our opinion of her at the moment.

Gisela, the first grader, has Fräulein Wesenberg as her teacher. By now, Fräulein Wesenberg must have gotten used to teaching little kids, because she is not so rigidly demanding anymore. According to Gisela, she is actually pretty nice. Also, Gisela doesn't have to write in the old German style very long, she learns cursive almost immediately.

One day, my sister comes home and tells us about the exciting day she has had in school.

"We all had to sing a song," she says. "Guess what I picked."

"What did you pick?" asks my mother.

"*Kum quae quase motine.*"

"Really?" My mother makes a disbelieving face. "And what did your teacher say to that?"

"*Kum quae quase motine*" is a fun song we have learned from Mama, I believe, or from Oma, maybe. Everybody in our family knows it. The lyrics to the happy tune are meaningless nonsense, and not many people are able to learn them. It's a bit difficult to remember so many strange words.

"My teacher liked it," says Gisela. "She took me from classroom to classroom, all through the school, and I had to sing it to all the kids."

When my mother happens to see the teacher in town, a few days later, the woman says, "Oh, Frau Beetz, you cannot imagine how happy I was when Gisela sang that song. I remember it from my youth. It brought back so many happy memories."

I have a feeling, Fräulein Wesenberg is rather fond of my mother, and she likes Gisela and me, too. Away from the classroom, she looks and acts just like someone's kind grandmother, but not like our own Oma, who is lively and a lot of fun.

*

The school year comes to an end. Gisela is promoted into second grade, and she is keeping the same teacher. I will go into fourth grade.

After a short spring break, I meet my new teacher. She is nice, but I have to get used to her ways. She has a habit of leaving the classroom for short periods of time, and we are expected to do our work as instructed. While she is out, we are not allowed to talk, and we have to stay in our seats. One kid is appointed temporary supervisor. He or she has to write down the names of offenders. I hate to be put in charge.

It soon turns out we have too many pupils in fourth grade, but fifth grade has a few openings. I, together with three others, am plucked from my class to jump into fifth. Only in math do I encounter a difficulty with long divisions, but my mother is willing to help me. She is good at explaining the material, and soon I am all caught up and doing just fine. Since I'm tall for my age and pretty mature in my thinking, I fit in with the bigger kids.

One day, Gisela brings home a picture drawn in school. She looks very pleased with her artwork, and Mama and I are supposed to admire it.

"What is it? A bag of flour?" asks my mother.

"Can't you see? It's Puss 'n' Boots!"

"Oh, of course."

Gisela seems relieved that Mama is able to recognize the cat.

A birthday is coming up. It's my mother's, on May 23. When Oma comes to visit the week before, she takes us shopping for birthday presents. We can afford to spend some money, for we have saved a small amount in our piggy banks.

"I want to buy three cups and saucers for Mama," announces my sister.

"Are you sure? Three of each?" asks Oma.

"Yes, I'm sure."

So we go to the store in town, and Gisela picks out three cups and three matching saucers. Oma carries them to the lady at the cash register, who quickly rings up the purchase.

"That will be ..." The woman names the price.

Gisela shakes her head.

"What's the matter?" asks Oma.

"If I give her this much money, I won't have any left."

"Should we put two cups and two saucers back?"

"No, I want to buy three of each."

Gisela holds on to her money.

"Let her pay for one set, and I will pay for the rest," Oma tells the saleswoman.

Gisela forks over the amount for one cup and one saucer, but happily proclaims she's bought all six pieces. I add three more sets to the purchase, for which I pay with my own money. We let Oma carry the well-wrapped bundles home. China is fragile, and she is more careful than Gisela and I are.

Mama is delighted with the birthday presents we give her, and she doesn't get told about this little episode with Gisela at the store until years later. Then we all have a good laugh.

*

As soon as summer vacation starts, Mama, Gisela and I are off to the Baltic again. We room upstairs in the big house like the year before, and we already think of the place as our second home. Everything is so familiar. We love it.

Though we don't eat our meals at Schössow's anymore, we still use the shortcut off and on. The geese don't pay attention to us, and the big dog remembers us from previous years. He wags his tail. We could probably go up to him and give him a little petting, but we prefer not to do so. A few friendly words while passing by have to do.

Though the war is on, summer guests still crowd the beach, but those guests are mainly women, children, and older men. If a young man is spotted, he has to be either on furlough or something is wrong with him, physically or mentally, to be exempted from the draft.

Sometimes, the mothers exchange experiences about life without their husbands and the hardships of the times. "When will this madness end?" is their question.

Since we have been in Neuendorf several summers in a row now, we have learned quite well how to provide for our daily needs the economic way. Blueberries are there for the picking. Basic groceries are available in a tiny store by Schössow's restaurant. Fresh vegetables and eggs can be bought, on certain mornings, right from a farm, at the edge of our village, on the main road that leads to Misdroy, the spa, the place those people frequent who want their vacations to be a bit more exciting. Meat, what little rations we are allowed, comes from the butcher in Kolzow, the inland village that has no tourists. It can be reached via shortcut through the woods. A baker has his shop in the vicinity of the path to the beach, and fishermen sell their catch right from their boats, very early in the morning.

Marie Teetzen goes mushroom picking, and she shows us the precious finds in her basket. "These, *Steinpilze* (ceps), grow by the stands of trees along the road to Warnow," she says, pointing to a knobby kind. "And those came from the deep woods. They are called *Pfifferlinge*, chanterelles. You can only find them in certain places. Nobody will ever give away the secret location where those rare, precious fungi

123

grow. In fact, if a mushroom picker goes to check up on them, he or she will always make sure that no one is following."

Since it's such a big secret, we don't pry. We just look and marvel.

Frau Teetzen also shows us a few other kinds; among them is the big umbrella mushroom. She describes their characteristics, and she tells us where to locate these obviously ordinary sorts.

So, one day, Mama, Gisela and I go to look for mushrooms along the road that leads to Warnow. Shortly behind the lake, on a little slope with the woods behind, we find some that look exactly like the knobby ones we have seen in Frau Teetzen's basket. For safety, my mother shows them to her.

"So, where did you come across them?" asks Marie Teetzen.

"In that area alongside the road which you told me about," says my mother.

"No good." Our landlady shakes her head and frowns. "You can throw them all away." Then she dumps the mushrooms we have been so proud to bring home.

We are disappointed.

"I think she didn't want us to butt into her territory." Now it is Mama's turn to shake her head. But instead of frowning, she just grins, shrugs, and says to us, "Anyhow, we really didn't come here to spend our precious vacation looking for mushrooms. We want to enjoy the beach and the water. Right?"

Gisela and I agree.

In no time at all, we have grabbed our paraphernalia and are on our way to the beautiful sea. We are so very, very lucky that we can spend our summer vacation far away from the daily reminders of war. In Neuendorf, all is serene. No sirens interrupt our sleep; no bombs threaten our safety.

Our four weeks of total peace disappear so quickly, and then it is time to pack up and return home. Soon, it is back to the old trot. School, homework, lights on only when the black window shades are down.

*

The news reports are encouraging. All is well on the western front. Our troops are said to be successful in their invasion of Russia. Onkel Willi sends letters from Russia to Tante Lotte, off and on to Mama, too. Nobody tells Gisela and me what news they contain.

Papa writes from France, and he still sends lots of pictures. He works one of those airplane detection apparatuses, which looks like a clumsy telescope. When he spots an enemy plane, he reports the coordinates to the gunners, who then aim their cannons in that direction and fire. For every successful hit, the cannon gets a ring painted on its barrel. If it weren't for the watchful eyes of men like my father and the skilled gunners, more bombs would fall on Berlin. I can understand that. But I fear for Papa's safety, and I know that Mama worries even more.

We usually go to bed early in order to get as much sleep as possible before the awful sound of the siren comes on. Sometimes, we have barely hit the pillow before we get chased out of bed again. Getting dressed is almost automatic now. We can do it in record time, for we have had plenty of practice.

During the night, when searchlights cross the sky and try to compete with the luster of stars, and the flames from burning buildings shine brighter than the moon, we know we are at war. But then, a number of hours later, the sun rises and the birds begin their morning song. It is peaceful. Nature does not care whether nations are foolishly warring or not.

*

Late summer walks to school, on the path that leads through the yellow fields of grain, are pleasant, even after nights without enough sleep. I would like to tarry and pick pretty flowers, which are growing everywhere, along the roadside and among the rows of wheat, oats, and rye. But I have to keep on going, for being late for school would mean a tongue lashing from the teacher. On the way home, in the company of other kids, laughing and talking, I don't remember to stop for posies.

During harvest time, we are off from school again. This is our fall break. Youngsters in the country, living on farms, are needed in the fields. They have to help bring in the crops. City children don't dig potatoes; they don't stack bundles of wheat, do the threshing or fill the hayloft; they don't even have to stoop to collect tons of apples from the ground. No, we city slickers and suburbanites are simply on vacation, or we do little chores to help our mothers in the house and in the garden, provided we have a plot that's cultivated.

Our garden is pretty much done by the time fall vacation comes around, but we also have to look after the lot on Fleischerstraße. Though we keep it mainly as grassland, the few planted trees and bushes need attention, off and on.

Fall is also a good time to make the long trip to Schildow, district of Oranienburg, which is situated just outside of Berlin, clear across from where we live. We own a piece of property there. Papa has bought it from his uncle, a builder, before his marriage to Mama. In order to get to Schildow, we take the trolley into Berlin. Then we transfer to a city train. At the end of the line, we wait for another train, a small one, which doesn't run very often, and that takes us the rest of the way. Honestly, it is quite a journey.

When we travel to Schildow, we always visit our relatives. They live in the center of that very small municipality, on the second floor of a house, which I believe belongs to them. The first floor is rented out to a baker. Behind the house is a long, but rather narrow garden, in which Gisela and I love to spend our time. All the way in the back are chickens, fenced in, and some cute rabbits. Lots and lots of vegetables grow in the center of the garden, and on the sides are beautiful flowers. Everything is neatly laid out and so very well kept. We may eat of the berries, if we visit during the right season, and the trees, loaded with apples, beckon to be raided. Our aunt usually serves us wonderful sandwiches with homemade lunchmeats, and she offers us cakes, which are excellent, too. I remember, years before, when Papa has been along, the uncle showing us his smoke chamber filled with sides of bacon and sausages of various sizes. I can still recall the tantalizing, mouthwatering, absolutely heavenly aroma of that smoked meat.

The velvet cloth on the dining room table fascinates Gisela. She strokes it as if it were a cat. I am more interested in the good food.

Our relatives live on the main road. To get to our property, we have to go to a strip of woods, turn left, and then walk a short distance until we reach Triftweg. As soon as we come to that corner, Gisela and I run to our meadow. We plop down by the trees and inhale the wonderful fragrance of sun-baked grasses and pine needles.

Triftweg is still a rather undeveloped section with only a house here and there. I love to visit the place. It is like being on a mini vacation.

Sometimes, we take a walk into the woods and locate the lake, which is rather hidden. It looks enchanted. I love it when the water lilies are in bloom. Off and on, fish are jumping out of the water and into the air. We also see water snakes and lots of frogs. It is too bad that we cannot linger. Time goes by so fast, and the way home is long. We have to get back to Rudow before dark, before the bombs begin to fly.

*

Second grade is shifted to the Wildmeisterdamm School. Now Gisela and I can walk together. Why this switch happens, I don't know. Perhaps, the old school in Rudow experiences overcrowding. Do we have too many kids in town?

Our *Führer*, for years, has urged German women to bear more children. Before the onset of the war, Mama's doctor has demanded to know, why she refuses to become pregnant again. She has produced two healthy daughters; she should have more. Repeatedly, she has been made to feel as if she were committing a crime against the state.

"I almost died having the last one," she says when someone mentions the subject now. "I actually had to defend myself."

I really don't know what has gotten into the older boys lately. They are always picking on the girls. Sometimes it's hard to get through the school day without being threatened.

"Fight back," says my mother. "Don't let them know you are afraid."

Is this Mama talking, the one who has always taught Gisela and me not to fight with each other?

The one who wouldn't even let us raise our voices or say a bad word?

I test the effectiveness of my newly given empowerment immediately. When boys hold the door shut to prevent us girls from passing from one school wing to the other, I walk, without flinching, toward the group and demand, with a voice of authority, "Open the door. Let us through." It works like a charm. The boys step aside. My friends and I, unhindered, are on our way to the other side of the building.

Also, the path through the fields isn't safe anymore. Bullies are trying to waylay us. A group of girls clusters around me, for now I'm considered their fearless leader.

"If you're trying to do something to us, you're in trouble," I say, giving the mean-looking boys an even meaner stare. "I'm going to knock you all down."

Then I hold my school bag in such a way that it is ready for swinging.

The boys, silent now, let the whole group of girls pass by.

Gisela is supposed to stay with me on the way home, but one day, she is nowhere to be found. I suspect she has slipped past without me noticing it, and now she is already way ahead and will beat me to the house. When I get home, she isn't there. Where could she be?

My mother is upset. She paces the floor. Then she goes to the gate and looks up and down the street … and paces some more. And I feel guilty.

About half an hour later, Gisela arrives, crying. It turns out that she and her little friend have been dawdling.

"Evchen was gone. We were afraid to walk across the field."

Big sobbing follows, and a lot of sniffling.

"We walked … to the corner … and took the streetcar … and then … we walked the other way home."

"But how did you ride the streetcar without money?" Mama wants to know.

"My friend had some. She paid."

"Don't ever do it again. Stay with your sister."

Mama sounds angry. She's not happy with Gisela. And I'm in trouble, too, I assume.

It is a blessing that the boys soon lose interest in trying to make life miserable for the girls. Perhaps, a parent has complained, and the evildoers have been called to the principal's office for punishment. Or, maybe, the ringleader has moved out of the area. Or the boys simply have found something more interesting to do with their time. Whatever the reason, the sexes exist peacefully side-by-side, at least for the time being.

*

Gisela and I still spend our free time in the safe confines of our garden. On rare occasions, Ursula, the big girl from down the street comes to visit for a while, and then we shoot marbles or spin the top.

131

Ursula is a much better marble shooter than I am.
Being a few years older, she has had lots more
practice. She always wants me to play my best
marbles, and then she wins them from me. After
losing several of my fancy ones, the agates, I get
upset. *No more of that,* I think. Then I take my
favorite marbles out of the bag and leave them in the
house.

"I know you have better ones than these," Ursula
says after careful inspection of my bag's content.
"What did you do with them?"

I refuse to give out information.

Ursula, her nose turned up in a snit, leaves.

Gisela and I play marbles for fun, not for keeps.
We admire our pretty glass marbles, hold them
against the light, and we cannot decide, which color
swirls we like best. The extra large ones, which we
call *Buckers,* are our special treasures, and we guard
them well. For simple shooting, the ordinary, drab
marbles work as well as the fancies. When one of
those gets lost, it is no tragedy. But Ursula only
wants to fill her bag with my pretty marbles, and
she's not getting any more.

Spinning the top is an art that has to be practiced.
Not only does the top have to be set twirling, it also
needs to be kept going and driven along. For the
driving part, a whip is required. First, the string gets
wound around the colorful top, all the way. Then,
very quickly, the stick has to be yanked away, pulling
the string off the top. This, if done correctly, sets the
top in motion. The little toy spins and spins, and

before it begins to teeter, the whip is being used. An expert can make the top travel for a long time. I'm trying hard, and I make my spinning top go a distance, but I'm certainly not an expert.

Another one of Gisela's and my favorite toys now is the wooden hoop, best used up and down the path that leads to the gate by the road. This is good exercise, because we have to run at a steady pace. To keep the hoop going, we need to hit it with a short, wooden stick. If we're not fast enough, our *Reifen* teeters and falls to the ground.

When the weather is too miserable for outdoor activities, we play with our dolls. My Inge and Gisela's Ingrid have to be mothered, but our tiny family, the one that lives in the dollhouse, remains our favorite. Sometimes, we get a board game out, like Chutes and Ladders or Parcheesi, or Chinese checkers. Mama joins us in those games, off and on, and we like that. She still sings with us, only not as often as before the war.

*

Winter arrives. The walk to school is a cold one. When we have to trudge through the snow, our feet feel like frozen pieces of meat, and our fingers get so cold, they lose all feeling. If the snow is still falling, we arrive in school looking like snow people.

Outside the classroom, all along the hallway, long, wooden boards are mounted, and screwed into them are many hooks. This is where we hang our coats, scarves and hats. The woolen mittens, when they are wet, get put on the floor. If we are lucky, everything will be dry by the time we have to bundle up again for the walk home. But our cold, wet shoes have to remain on our feet for the whole school day. On those miserable winter days, getting home and changing into dry stockings and a fresh pair of warm socks is the most satisfying moment of the day. Oh, it feels so good to put the feet near the black iron heater that has a nice fire burning inside. And when Mama offers hot chocolate and, perhaps, a baked apple, heaven couldn't be much better.

Another Christmas approaches. It's almost the end of 1941, a bit more than two years into the war, and no end of the strife is in sight. I hear that more countries have taken up arms, but I don't know all of them. There are so many. Japan does something somewhere. China is involved. And the United States of America! Why do we have to get mixed up with America, the country that's all the way across the ocean?

Gisela amuses us once more. She has a tiny notebook into which she has written what she wants to give everyone for Christmas. Mama and I almost split our sides laughing when we read her entries. The list, made out in childish handwriting, is long. For me, she has at least eight gifts in mind. "And that's enough for Evchen," is written at the bottom of that list. She also intends to be quite generous with presents for Mama. All the relatives are supposed to get something. Now we are eager to find out what she's going to do. Will she ask Oma to go shopping with her like she has done for my mother's birthday in May? I don't think Oma is going to fall for that one again.

Christmas arrives, and we get nothing from Gisela. Of course, she has no money at her disposal.

"It is the thought that counts," Mama says. I agree.

Oh, my little sister is so precious.

*

In 1942, the bombings intensify, not only in Berlin, but also all over Germany. Targeted are the industrial cities, mainly those that have factories valuable to the war effort, power plants, and transportation centers.

We are invited to take shelter in a neighbor's large basement a few houses down the street. But from the moment the sirens begin to wail to when the bombs start to fall, even if we hurry, we often can't get under cover fast enough. We try running to this big shelter on a few occasions, and then we give up. Tante Lotte's tiny cellar is much more convenient. With a direct hit, neither place would be safe.

No matter where we go during an air raid, Mama carries her most important papers. In her handbag is the usual stuff, wallet, identification papers, ration cards, and whatever else a woman carries, but in that other pouch, the one she has sewn herself, are the official books with her and Papa's family registers. *Stammbuch* is the name for such a book, and it holds the legal entries of births, baptisms, marriages, and deaths. Every newlywed couple is given such a book. Mama has all the information about the Krause family in her book, and Papa has the Beetz family data. A legally authorized person makes the entries, and everything has a notary seal. No separate birth certificate is ever required, and no long death certificate is issued.

I find it interesting to read the listings in the *Stammbuch*. Oma's maiden name is Rupprecht. That's the name of St. Nicholas's servant. The saint and his *Knecht Rupprecht,* or *Ruprecht,* are the ones who bring sweets to good children on December 6.

The last name of one of Opa's forebears is Weihnacht, meaning Christmas. Now that's what I call a coincidence!

Mama has stressed the importance of the two books, repeatedly. "Never lose them. They are of great value. We need them for life."

Where would I lose them? I never take them anywhere. Of course, I do not realize that, way down the road, I, the oldest child, will become the keeper of those books that hold the family records.

*

In no time at all, winter is over. The end of fifth grade is in sight. Now it is time for me to get registered for high school. But … only students coming out of fourth grade can make the switch to middle school or high school. The law is the law, and there's no getting around it.

Students have a choice. They may go to elementary school for eight years straight and then find an apprenticeship to learn a trade. While getting on-the-job training, they have to take a certain number of classes per week, for two years, relevant to their future occupation. Or, after fourth, they may attend middle school, for six more years. For an even better education, parents send their children to the mandatory elementary school for four years, and then let them go to high school for another eight. College may follow.

Mama, who still harbors a great bitterness because her parents have refused her a high school education, is adamant that Gisela and I will have better schooling. Of course, times have changed since she has been a young girl. "A girl doesn't need all that book learning. High school is for boys," her father has supposedly said. "Girls learn something practical, like dress making." A nursing career would have been more to my mother's liking.

Papa has gotten his high school diploma, and then he has gone on to college to study business management. He has also learned the art of making combs, not just those for everyday use, but also the very decorative ones, with intricate patterns, like the elegant ladies wear in their hair. Großer Opa has owned a comb factory until the era of the great depression, and the idea, at that time, has been that Papa should manage the company. But like so many other businesses, Groβer Opa's has not been able to survive the bad times. No more comb factory, no need for a manager. I guess that's why my father has opened his own little business, selling candies and newspapers and tobacco wares. Groβer Opa has had a bar for a while, after the loss of his factory. "He always dressed in a suit and a tie, like a real gentleman," the aunts tell. "And that in a working class neighborhood! No wonder his customers left."

I really don't know why people make fun of others. Groβer Opa is such a nice man, and, at least, he has let Papa get his education, which Mama says is so very important.

In order to enter high school in the spring, I have to be demoted. So, back into fourth grade I go, back to my old friends, and back to easier textbooks.

The nearest high school is in Britz. I have to walk to the corner where Papa's kiosk has been and then take the trolley. My public transit pass, paid for by the month, allows me to transfer twice. I only use the transfers when the weather is bad; otherwise I walk part of the way.

My school is located in the old village section of Britz. It's a charming area with cobblestone streets, big, ancient trees, and mostly country-style houses in pretty gardens, behind picket or meshed wire fences. Across the street from our school is the *Britzer Dorfkirche* (Village Church of Britz), the Protestant church, Lutheran denomination, which dates back to the 1300s. Shaded by old trees, it sits behind a huge stonewall. Entrance to the grounds is through a tall, ornate, wrought iron gate. A brick path leads to the massive main church door.

Abutting the church property, to the left, is a lovely park, in the center of which is a pond, the *Britzer Dorfteich*. Weeping willows bend their branches into the water at one end, and this is the favorite spot for ducks to build their nests. Mama has gone skating on this lake, as a young girl, wearing ice skates borrowed from a girlfriend. "It has been great fun," she tells us, "and I had always wished to own skates of my own."

Gisela and I don't have skates. Rudow has no lake, no little pond, not even a stream. So … what's the sense of wasting money on something that cannot be used? But whenever we find a frozen puddle, we slide across it wearing our regular shoes, hoping that Mama doesn't find out about it.

Now back to my new school's surroundings. To the left of the park with the pond, across another cobblestone street is the *Britzer Schloss*, a castle, which is surrounded by a huge park. This castle doesn't have turrets and a moat like those built for kings and other royalty. It looks no grander than an enormous mansion.

My high school occupies a little triangle surrounded by the church, the park belonging to the castle, and by yet another park. This other park is called the *Rosenpark*, so named for its many roses. Honestly, it's a lovely location for our school.

The two-storied high school building is old. Papa has already received his education in it – with the

139

same principal, our *Herr Direktor,* in charge. But I believe the side wing, where the music room and the bathrooms are located, doesn't date back quite that far.

The schoolyard is big enough for ballgames. If we need to do track and field sports or use the gym, we have to trudge to the newer school, located several blocks away.

I'm not fond of ballgames, because the ball is so hard, and I'm afraid of getting hurt. Track and field, I love. I can run like the wind, and I am able to jump far. High jump is good, too. The apparatus in the gym is for the students in higher grades, I assume. But we are allowed to use the mats for tumbling and other floor gymnastics. I can do tumbling. Cartwheels, headstands, handstands, splits … forget it! Nobody has ever taught me how to do those tricks. Most of the other girls can do them. Some of my classmates are talented; others do a fair job. For some unknown reason, the teacher only tests us once and then forgets about floor exercises for the rest of the year. I am greatly relieved. On my first report card, she writes, "Despite physical weakness, Eva is doing a great job." Mama, when she reads this, has a good laugh. She knows that her tall and skinny daughter is full of strength and energy.

*

High school is much more demanding than fifth grade. For each subject, we have a different teacher.

Now I have to get used to the expectations of many instructors, not only one.

Math is fine. I love to work with numbers. And, besides, some of what is being taught I've already had the previous year. German, my native language subject, is a different story. The reading, spelling, and grammar parts present no problem, and neither does the homework. But my first composition in class is an absolute disaster.

I have always been a good storyteller. My essays have pleased all my teachers, from grade one to five. But ...since I've never been allowed to hand in a sloppy assignment, I'm used to writing everything on scratch paper first. Then I edit. When it's all corrected and beautiful sounding, I copy it, carefully, to the good sheet of paper, the one that goes to the teacher. This procedure takes time, but it has been worth it ... so far.

Now this new teacher comes along and puts on the blackboard – I can still hear the screeching of the chalk as she prints, in bold letters: MY TRIP TO THE ZOO. Then she gives us fifteen minutes to write a report about yesterday's outing to see the monkeys and the bears and the tigers and the elephants and so much more. Fifteen minutes? How can I possibly put something worthwhile on paper in such a short time? For sure, I'll make mistakes, if I don't write on scratch paper first. I'll have to make corrections. Ink erasures look bad. Cross something out? That's horrible! The clock ticks; my paper is still blank. I feel sick. Finally, a few sentences appear on my paper. They are no better than coming from a second grader. I could cry; that's how ashamed I am. When the reports are handed back, I receive my very first bad mark, equivalent to a big, fat D. Needless to say, I hate to show this to my mother.

We now have history, and it's purely present-day political. Göbbels. Born when? Where? What has he done in his youth? How has he risen to his leadership position? What about Göhring, Himmler, and all the other Nazi bigwigs? My head is swimming with dates and places and job descriptions. Oh, how I hate this subject! One day, the teacher picks on me, and I don't know the answer. "I don't care what these men did," I foolishly blurt out. He gives me a dirty look and says nothing. As long as we learn about Hitler's elite, I get no more chances to answer questions in history class. I could easily have been hauled out of school, my whole family could have been accused of being anti-Nazi, and who knows what might have befallen all of us. I am blissfully unaware of the danger. For that marking period, I get a D in history on my report card. It is my only really, really bad grade, thank God. The one for German comes out to a C, which, in my opinion, is a disgrace, too.

My very first day in English class is a bit scary. To introduce us to the new language, our very nice teacher speaks only in that foreign tongue, and I don't understand a word of what she is saying. She points to the wall and to the window and to so many other objects, and then she says the words for all those things. We have to repeat them, but they don't want to stick in my poor head.

Totally confused, I come home that day and tell Mama about my new experience.

"Wall, window, table, chair. Is this what your teacher said? Lamp, perhaps?"

"How do you know?" I ask my mother. "You never had English."

"Tante Klärchen took a course once, and she taught me a few words." Mama beams. She seems so very proud that she is able to help me with English on that first day of my foreign language study.

It turns out that English isn't hard at all. I love it. Besides math, it's my favorite subject. Perhaps, it's even better than math.

Geography is a bit boring. We have to remember which area of Germany is industrial and which one specializes in agriculture. Wheat grows here, something else there. Coal comes mainly from a certain area, but also from another part of the country. Iron, copper, zinc, and a multitude of other ores are found … where? Oh, for goodness sakes, this is so complicated! I would much rather memorize long poems or a list of English vocabulary than statistics of riches from the soil or from deep in the mountains. But learning about German regions and what they prosper from is better than finding out about all those high-ranking men in uniforms that are covered with braids, ribbons, and rows of shiny medals.

I know a little verse, recited by some grownups, but I'm not allowed to say it in public. Perhaps, I shouldn't even say it at all, just for safety. It's one of those things that can get you into serious trouble. *"Lametta, Lametta, der Bauch wird immer fetter."* Translated, it means: "Tinsel, tinsel, the belly constantly gets fatter." Shiny decorations, in this case Hermann Göhring's, are referred to as tinsel. I even forget who has explained this to me. It may have been Oma, for she is the one who loves to say things with hidden meanings.

Once a week, a woman comes to teach us religion. She reads us nice Bible stories, and then we talk about them. Getting an A in religion is a snap. Anybody can ace that class, I think.

Art is easy, too. I've enjoyed drawing and painting since my very early days. Art classes are always so relaxing.

It is quite the contrary, at times, when it comes to our music lessons. They can be extremely exciting, especially when our teacher practices notes with us. He has the scale written on the board. Whoever he calls by name has to stand up and sing the note or a series of notes our teacher points to with his stick. Good luck! Most of the kids have not the slightest idea what a "C" or a "G" sounds like. Honestly, nobody has ever taught us to read music in grade school, and only a few youngsters are taking piano lessons or play another instrument for which they have to recognize notes. And so our dear teacher has to listen to more wrong sounds than correct

144

ones, and it makes him furious. He clenches his fists; his face takes on the expression of a gargoyle; he plops his skinny behind down on his chair, grabs his over-the forehead-tumbled, longish hair as if to pull it out, and then he stomps his feet. What a performance! The majority of my classmates are scared stiff, I believe. Some sit expressionless and wait for our teacher's outburst to pass. I think it's hilarious. Of course, if I would be the one responsible for his attacks of utter madness, I might cringe, too. But, for some reason, after just a few lessons, I'm pretty good at finding the correct notes. Singing makes me happy. It runs in the family.

*

Just as I've gotten used to the peculiarities of my new teachers, summer vacation comes along again. As in previous years, Mama, Gisela, and I travel to the Baltic, where, in Neuendorf, our familiar accommodations are waiting for us. Truly, this has become our home away from home. By now, though, I wish that, for a change, we could spend a few weeks somewhere else, like in the mountains, for instance. I've never seen the mountains except in pictures. They look so beautiful, so majestic, with snowcaps up on top. Even a hilly area might do for starters, something with little peaks and perhaps an old castle here and there.

I've read *Heidi*, the book by Johanna Spiri, and the description of the Alps has made me want to see

145

them for myself. But Mama is infatuated with the sea, and Gisela is a total water rat. She likes nothing better than to frolic in the water. Gisela, I believe, already takes summers in Neuendorf for granted. Of course, I like it there, too, but still …

Something very good is happening during this year's vacation. Papa is up for his furlough. He is allowed to spend two whole, glorious weeks with us. Gisela and I don't mind that we have to crawl into bed together so that Papa can have the one I usually sleep in. We would gladly do this for the rest of our lives, if we could only keep him with us and not have to send him back to France, into the war.

"It's about time you learn to swim," my father says to us when we arrive at the beach. Then he demonstrates the breaststroke. "It's like bicycle riding. You can't stop. When you don't move your arms and legs, you'll sink. And when you want to stop, you just let one foot come down until it touches the bottom."

Then Papa takes turns holding Gisela and me under the belly and chest to keep us up, and he encourages us to do the movements correctly. "Don't forget the legs," he keeps reminding us. "And don't forget to breathe."

I believe my sister is learning to swim much faster than I. She has lots of confidence, and she doesn't mind when water gets in her face. I hold my head real high. When, by accident, water comes in my eyes, nose, or mouth, I panic. I guess I'm like Mama. She never goes out far, and her head is always completely above water. When Papa ventures into the deep, she fears for his safety. He laughs at her.

*

It is 1942, and I'm ten years old. By law, I now have to be a member of Hitler's youth organization. I have to become a *Jungmädel* (Young Girl). For indoctrination, I am ordered to go to a meeting that takes place on the athletic field across from where Papa has sold his wares. A black, straight skirt and a white, short-sleeved blouse have to be worn. Mama quickly sews a skirt for me, and we go to the store to buy a blouse. All I can remember about this meeting on a hot summer day is that a big group of girls my age are standing around, waiting for their names to be called. We are all bored as a speaker, in full uniform, talks to us, and we can hardly wait to be dismissed.

"You will be notified about further meetings," we are told.

Since no notification arrives, I quickly forget about the whole business, and my new skirt and blouse take up valuable space in our closet.

The news from the eastern front is encouraging. The German army is penetrating deeper into southern Russia. But closer to home, the situation isn't quite so good. Now the Americans have joined the British in the dropping of bombs. The planes arrive from England at night, and bombs fall wherever factories and other important targets are

147

suspected. During the day, American bombers do a more precise job. They hit specific targets without damaging too much of the surrounding areas.

Bad news comes from Russia about a big battle at Stalingrad. The enemy won't budge. Still, hope exists everything will turn out well. So we are told.

"Oh, I do hope that Onkel Willi is not among the troops fighting there," says my mother. "Nobody has heard from him. We don't know where he is."

*

I believe it is in the fall of 1942 when we visit Tante Klärchen, Mama's sister, in a village near Güstrow, in the state of Mecklenburg. She and her new husband have a little farm there. Everybody calls my new uncle by his last name, Petchak, and I don't think I've ever heard anybody mention his first name. Besides a bit of farming, he makes and fixes wagon wheels.

The best thing about this brief, absolutely boring visit in the Güstrow area is playing with the cats. When Gisela and I sit on the front steps of the thatched-roof farmhouse, those cats always come running, and then they rub their heads and their slinky bodies against our legs, thus asking to be petted. They thank us with their loud purrs.

Across the dirt yard, by the barn, a dog is tied up. Perhaps he would like some attention, too, but we don't go near him. Nobody tells us, if this dog is friendly or not.

It smells like barnyard, like pigs and cows and manure pile, and my nose doesn't like it. "I will never marry a farmer," I declare.

I don't think my aunt is very happy in this country environment. It's so very isolated, and she doesn't seem to have friends. Also, she's not the kind who likes to take care of animals in the barn and free-range chickens that leave droppings all over the yard. Tante Klärchen is a rather delicate woman, suited for a city apartment with a few flowers in the windows and on the balcony and, perhaps, a little canary in a cage, but not for an old farmhouse, far away from all friends and family and only her radio inside and cackling and grunting outside to listen to all day until her husband comes home, and he's not very talkative.

"No, no, I'll never marry a farmer," I keep repeating.

As far as I know, Mama, Gisela and I are the only relatives who ever visit Tante Klärchen while she lives in that village. Her brothers, even if they should be interested, can't go to her, because they all have to fight a war, and their short visits home are spent with their wives in Berlin. Oma and Opa, I believe, would never think of taking the train to see their daughter. And, besides, they don't seem to like Petchak very much, for he's a plain man and so unlike Karl, Tante Klärchen's first husband, the supposedly very handsome, charming women chaser.

149

"Not fair," says Mama. "Petchak is a decent man. He's a hard worker. And, at least, he's not running around like the other one."

I don't remember seeing much of Achim, my cousin. He's fifteen years old and may have an apprenticeship already. But, one day, we do have a lot of fun with him. He takes us to the big pile of hay in the barn, and then we all jump into the sweet-smelling, dusty, dried grass, pretending it is a cool pool of water.

Mama sews dresses for Tante Klärchen while we are visiting. Mama always sews dresses for all the female relatives, and sometimes she gets frustrated. Off and on, she says to Gisela and me, "I would never let you become a dressmaker, because then all the women in the family and your friends expect you to sew clothes for them. They think you have nothing else to do."

She never complains about making clothes for Oma. In fact, I believe, she likes to make her mother look pretty. Oma almost always gets blue dresses, usually navy blue, with a small, white flower or polka dot print, and a white collar, either with or without lace, or all lace. My grandmother looks so beautiful in those dresses.

*

November 1942. The news reports are really bad. First, we hear that the Allied Forces have landed in North Africa. Our Field Marshall Rommel is in Africa

150

with his troops. He's called the Desert Fox. A few days later, the Russians begin a counter-attack at Stalingrad. Still, there has to be hope for a German victory. The *Führer* says so.

In January 1943, matters look even bleaker. Apparently, the round faced man from England, the one with the cigar in his mouth, whose name is Churchill, meets with Roosevelt, the American, in Casablanca, which is in Africa, and the two of them want Germany to give up. Immediately after that, the news reports tell us that the Americans have launched an attack on Germany, in the west, at Wilhelmshaven. And, for goodness sakes, things go terribly bad in Russia, too. One of the divisions of the German Army capitulates at Stalingrad; our troops are pulling back. Joseph Göbbels, in his big February speech from the Sports Palace in Berlin, still sounds as if this is only a temporary setback, and he says we have to fight a total war. We will not give up. Germany will not be defeated. I wonder what a total war is supposed to be like. Fighting is all around us. So many nations are involved. Nobody talks of quitting. This cannot be just half a war. What more does Göbbels want?

Mama is very worried.

The bombings are awful. More and more houses are in ruins, especially toward the center of Berlin. A few times, we go to a real bunker, a very large, strong one, but it is a distance away. Though we hurry, there are not enough minutes to reach that steel and concrete shelter before the enemy planes are overhead. Mama is afraid we may get killed by an exploding bomb or hurt from flying debris. She also doesn't like to be trapped underground with so many strangers. So we keep on taking our chances in Tante Lotte's flimsy cellar, which pleases my aunt.

*

In the spring of 1943, shortly after I've started the new school year, the evacuation of Berlin and other big cities begins. Tante Dora, who has a housekeeping job in a hospital, is sent to somewhere in Mecklenburg, together with patients, nurses, and doctors. Her sister, Tante Kaethe, a secretary in a military office, has already been out of the city for a while. Groβer Opa, who now works for Lorenz, an electrical appliance company, well known for its radios, gets moved to Mittweida, a small town in Saxony. Tante Gertrud, recently pregnant with child, packs her bags and moves in with her parents in Landeck, the place of that memorable wedding celebration several years ago.

Tante Lotte decides to weather the bomb attacks in her own home. Oma and Opa wouldn't think of leaving Berlin.

My mother will get in contact with our Neuendorf landlords to find out, if they are willing to let us have our little vacation apartment for a while, until the bombs stop falling. But before arrangement for the big move can be made, I'm already being shipped out to Bansin, which is one of the spas on the island of

Usedom, situated in the Baltic Sea next to Wollin, "our" island, the place of so many lovely summer vacations.

*

All the girls of the lower grades from my high school, whose parents sign the agreement, are being evacuated to Bansin, and some of our teachers accompany us. The boys have a different destination, but I have no idea which part of the country has been selected for them.

I have no recollection of the farewell. Am I afraid to go on an uncertain journey without Mama and Gisela? Or do I take it calmly, confident that I will be reunited with them in a very short time, just as soon as they settle in Neuendorf? Or am I hardened so much already by all the nightmares of the war that I'm not capable of fear and feeling sorry for myself?

I also don't remember anything about how we get to Bansin. It must've been by train. How else? But I'm able to bring back a picture of our arrival at the hotel, our home away from home.

We are all assembled in the big center yard, with the luggage by our side. A grownup calls out names and room assignments. Someone leads us, in groups, to our building – there are three – and the correct wing. I end up in a pleasant, airy room with a view to the street and the woods beyond. My bed is by the window, which pleases me.

One of my roommates is a girl my age. Though we have not been in the same class in Berlin, I have seen

153

her before. We get along well. The other girl is a year younger, and she is not quite so friendly. Perhaps, she is just shy around us older girls. We try to be nice to her, but she doesn't want to warm up to us. Also, she stinks – like a feral animal. No matter how much we keep the window open, the stench doesn't want to leave.

In our frustration, the good roommate and I throw hints, first subtle, then stronger, about body hygiene and clean clothes. They fall on deaf ears.

Finally, we talk to one of the counselors. That woman tells us, "Perhaps the girl suffers from some kind of ailment and cannot help it. Get used to it."

So our room smells as if a pack of wolves has taken up residence in it until, one day, the girl is moved somewhere else. Her bed remains empty.

For meals, we assemble in the big dining hall, where long tables have been put together. We take turns with setting up, bringing out food, and clearing the tables.

Breakfast is invariably a pink flour soup, like a watered-down strawberry pudding, with or without cookie or cake crumbs on top. I can only image that a local bakery provides us with those crumbs. We may have gotten something different off and on, like oatmeal, perhaps, but I can only remember that pink soup in my bowl.

Our main meals, served at lunchtime, vary from day to day. Often, we have soup, like at home, but not as tasty. Sometimes, we are treated to boiled potatoes, a bit of meat, and a vegetable on the side.

On Sundays, we have a piece of cake or cookies for dessert. That's where the crumbs might come from for the pink breakfast soups, I think, if not from the bakery.

One day, the kitchen staff has prepared a horrible meal for us. Clams or snails or whatever those little things on the plate are … how unappetizing!

We shove the despised stuff aside. We are found out.

"Finish everything on your plate. That's an order!"

I force myself to eat the strange tasting morsels. I shudder with every bite. I feel like throwing up.

Some of the girls defy the order. They absolutely refuse to even take one bite.

"Whoever doesn't finish, will get it for supper."

And then, really, a kitchen worker comes around with a big bowl and collects all the horrible leftovers, those round, ugly bits of fishy stuff. Back to the kitchen the whole mess goes.

For supper, all lunchtime delinquents have to line up by the kitchen counter, and they are meted out the detested grub. Am I glad that I get my regular sandwich! Dark bread with a bit of liverwurst scraped on suddenly tastes extra delicious.

We all have kitchen duties to perform. Sometimes, we peel potatoes, lots and lots of them. Or we help with the dishes. I don't mind doing the potatoes. Actually, it's a happy job, because when we girls sit in a circle, outdoors, around the huge pile of spuds and the big tub into which the peeled ones get thrown, we tell stories or jokes, or we sing, and we laugh a whole lot.

Once a week, we do our laundry, in that same area, in the back of the hotel property, where the potato peeling always takes place. A few tubs, close to the wall of the rear building, get filled with hot, sudsy water; others have clear, cold water for rinsing. We are assigned a certain day and time, according to room number. Since so many girls are living in the hotel, the clotheslines are filled every single day of the week except on Sunday. Germans don't hang their laundry out on Sundays. It would make a very bad impression. But they are allowed to put their bedding in the open window. That's a common practice. Pillows and bedcovers need the fresh- air smell, even on a Sunday. Doing laundry, however, is work, and you aren't supposed to labor on the seventh day.

Our school lessons do not suffer. Each morning, after the dining area has been cleaned up, tables and chairs get rearranged in clusters to accommodate various classes. Music and art are being taught upstairs, in separate rooms. Teachers, nurse, and administration occupy the rest of the top floor.

Our teachers, including the ones who have been so very strict while still in Berlin, are now gentle. Even our wild music teacher does not act up anymore. He never goes into another hair-pulling-feet-stomping performance. Honestly, he has transformed into the kindest, most caring father figure.

In our free time, we often go into the woods across the street, and we gather for songfests in a sunlit clearing. Oh, how I love those afternoons! Music makes me so happy. I even try to sing harmony. Most of the folksongs I already know, but I also learn a few new ones.

One day, our leader announces we are going to perform a play. It will combine acting, singing, and dancing. I will be in the chorus, which suits me just fine, because chorus members are busy throughout the musical.

The story, as I remember, goes something like this: Flowers go to sleep while the chorus is singing a soft slumber song. Then fairies arrive, fluttering, and they perform a dance in the moonlight. A wicked witch appears, grabs one of the fairies, and drags her away. All upset, and scared, the rest of the fairies run off to find the house of woodland elves. One of the little men comes out and listens to the sad tale of the kidnapping. Before he enlists his companions in the fairy-rescue effort, we watch the elves at work. They are tailors, but when their master is out, they stop wielding their needles and have fun. Then they jump over worktable and benches until the master returns. Of course, in the end, the abducted fairy is saved, and fairies and elves perform a happy dance together.

For our show in the woods, we invite the girls of another evacuation camp, and they give us thunderous applause. I believe this is the only time

157

we ever get together with kids from outside our hotel. Also, we are never led into town.

But, off and on, some teachers walk with us to the beach. We play ball in the sand and, when it's balmy enough, wade in the water. As midsummer comes along and the temperatures climb, the Baltic Sea warms up enough for us to go swimming. We usually stay close to the shore where our supervisors can keep a close eye on us. Not many of the girls know how to swim. Though Papa has taught me how the year before, I'm still not confident to go into deep water.

Mama sends me letters all the time, and I write back quite often. When I report that I like it in Bansin, I really mean it. Honestly, I'm happy in my new surroundings. I have lots of friends my own age here, the comradeship is great, our teachers treat us well, and the accommodations are comfortable. Woods and sea beckon. The sun shines most of the time.

Air raid sirens go off only occasionally, and since this disturbance usually happens during the day, our sleep is not interrupted. As far as I know, a bomb has destroyed not a single house in the area. Life is good.

One day, when the sirens wail again and we all march out into the woods across the street, in orderly fashion, it is far from our minds that our sense of security might become shattered. Since nothing has ever happened, we consider this hiding under the trees absolutely ridiculous. But it is a precaution. Our chaperones tell us that, if bombs are meant for the island, they will most certainly be dropped on houses and not on strips of woods. The thick canopy of leaves is there to hide us and so protect us from possible strafing.

Then it happens. Crash! Down comes a big tree, no more than perhaps twenty feet away from where we stand, huddled in small groups, a bunch of girls now too frightened to move for a few seconds … minutes … or what seems more like an eternity.

As we begin to scramble from the vicinity of that fallen giant of a tree, like a flock of birds disturbed by a sudden intruder, some here, some there, alone or by twos or threes, holding on to each other for assurance, broken branches come raining down, all around us.

When the shower of debris finally stops, one of our teachers blows a whistle, and then she orders us, in loud, authoritative voice, to come and gather around her.

It takes a while until the group is assembled. Some girls are still panting from running. Most are visibly shaken. A few have tears in their eyes.

We take a head count. All are present.

Above, we hear the enemy planes fly over the coastal area of Usedom.

"They must've dropped a bomb by accident," says the teacher. She's obviously trying to take away our fear of having to go through serious air raids like in Berlin.

As soon as the all-clear signal is given, we return to our corner of the big dining room, where our textbooks are still spread out, and we resume our lessons as if nothing bad has interrupted them. Our teacher must've guessed correctly. An accident, that's all it has been.

*

One morning, as we are in the middle of German class and the teacher explains an assignment to us, I begin to feel terribly woozy. I can barely understand what is being said, but I try to scribble down the instructions. A composition is due the following day.

I can't think. I can't keep my head up. It worries me … somewhat … like from a foggy distance. How am I supposed to get my writing done? "Just drift off," says my brain.

Somebody notices my condition and takes me upstairs to the nurse's office. There's a bed, and I am grateful to be allowed to plop down on it.

"You have badly infected tonsils and a high fever," says the nurse after checking me over. "We'll put you in the hospital for a few days, and they'll make you all better there."

How I get to the makeshift hospital in town, I cannot recall. But I do remember my relief of not having to bother with the German assignment.

By suppertime, after some pills and a good sleep, I feel well enough to eat the tasty, thin German pancakes, *Eierkuchen*. They remind me of home and my mother's cooking.

"Every sick girl brought in here gets pancakes for her first meal," explains one of my roommates. "After that, forget about such good stuff."

Too bad. I could eat those lovely pancakes every day.

After less than a week, I'm pronounced fit enough to be released. I'm still weak, though, and I could do with more bed rest.

That afternoon, our teachers take us to the beach. They let me go along. In fact, I'm allowed to put on my bathing suit and go swimming. Nobody suggests I should just sit on the beach or wade in the water. No, they let me go in all the way.

So I walk into the cold sea and do some swimming where it isn't deep. I put my feet down again and take a few steps to the side. Suddenly, I stumble into a big hole. The water goes over my head. I pop up and try to swim, but I can't. I go under again. Surfacing once more, I gasp for air, and I try to call for help. I don't think my voice is loud enough. Down I go again, and up I come, and the people not too far away from me don't seem to notice. Then it feels as if I'm gently gliding down, down, down. I hear music, beautiful music. The sounds that surround me are heavenly, like angel choirs. Oh, how peaceful it is.

I do not know how much time has passed, but when I awaken, I'm lying on the beach. People are clustered around me. But the first faces I recognize are those of my mother and Gisela. It's a miracle! Instead of being with the angels, I'm with my loved ones, right here on earth.

"We've come to take you home," says my mother. "To Neuendorf."

I'm a little confused. I guess it shows.

Then Mama explains. "We wanted to surprise you. The people at the hotel told us you were at the beach with the girls. And then this! We find you here, just pulled out of the water. Oh, my God!" She wipes away some tears, but then breaks out in a big, happy smile.

"We've been so scared," Gisela sobs. "I couldn't imagine losing my sister."

That same afternoon, after all my things are packed and the formalities taken care of, I say farewell to some of my friends and teachers, and then my sojourn in Bansin is over. I'm off to Neuendorf with Mama and Gisela.

*

Everybody can tell my sister is happy that we are now official residents of Neuendorf and not just summer guests as in years past. If it were up to her, I believe, she would spend the rest of her life in this little village. My mother is cheerful, too. I'm getting used to the idea of not returning to Berlin in the near future. Who knows how long this war is going to drag on and what might happen at the end of it. The newscasters proclaim nothing good, but the politicians speak of hope. In "our" village it is still peaceful enough.

One thing bothers my mother. The closest high school is in Misdroy, a distance away. She checks it out, but the only way I could attend this school would be as a boarding pupil. I am not in favor of going to a boarding school, Mama is not convinced this is a good idea, and, besides, it's too expensive. That settles the matter. Gisela and I will attend Neuendorf's tiny village school together.

We've never had it so convenient. The schoolhouse is just around the corner. No more walking across fields, no more riding the trolley, no more wondering if lessons begin at the regular hour or late due to bomb attacks after midnight.

Gisela and I start out in different classrooms, she in the one for the little kids, in the back of the building, and I am in the front room with the big boys and girls. Fifth graders sit in the front row; eighth graders are all the way in the back.

Our teacher, Herr Sydow, instructs the few students in the front row first. While they work on their assignments, he advances to the next group and then on and on. When the upper classes receive their instructions, I listen in. This keeps me from getting bored with my own simple lessons.

Gisela, during the first weeks, always comes home a nervous wreck. It's the fault of the teacher, Herr Sydow. He practices multiplication tables with the fourth graders. Like a drill sergeant, he shouts the numbers and then quickly points at his victim for the answer. Though Gisela knows her multiplications very well, she gets so scared that she cannot answer. Mama practices with her, using the same frightening method as our teacher. Eventually, Gisela develops immunity to the shouting and pointing, and her answers don't get stuck in her throat anymore.

Since I still have my books from Berlin, my mother insists I continue my high school lessons at home. She is determined that I will not fall behind. Somehow, she also finds out about an old, learned lady, evacuated here from Hannover, who speaks English, and she pays her a visit. Soon after that meeting, I go for weekly English lessons to the apartment of Frau Professor Michel – in exchange for my mother's coffee rations.

Frau Professor is a rather nice, refined, elderly lady, a bit on the plump side, with completely gray hair, pinned up in a bun. Her husband is friendly, too. Usually, after my lesson, the three of us sit together for a bit, and I have sweet tea and a slice of bread with sugar on top with them. I think they are rather fond of me.

A few months later, Frau Professor takes on two more students. Heino and Joff are twin brothers, about my age, but they don't look like twins at all. Dark Joff is much slighter than his blond brother. He lacks Heino's self-confidence, which makes him, on occasion, in my eyes, a bit of a sissy.

One evening, as we are walking home from our English lesson, Joff feels the urge to relieve his bladder.

"I can't wait till I get home," he moans.

"Then use a tree," suggests his brother.

"Okay."

Heino and I walk on, leaving Joff behind to do what he has to do.

"Don't leave me alone," wails the one by the tree. "I'm scared all by myself."

Heino and I walk back to keep the silly one company. I am embarrassed.

Sometimes, I wonder how Frau Professor puts up with the twins. They rarely know their lesson, and they invent the dumbest words. When they haven't studied their vocabulary, they simply try to make the German words sound English, and that is so very funny. Our teacher shakes her head, and then she reminds the two that they should really try to make more of an effort.

I believe the boys come from Stettin. Their parents are well off and can afford to rent rooms in the big manor up on the hill. The father is an older businessman and doesn't have to serve in the war. If he lives with them all the time or only comes to visit on weekends, I never find out. Actually, I don't even know what the boys' mother looks like. But I do learn that they have a maid. A maid? I've never before met anyone who has a maid.

*

All kinds of evacuees live in Neuendorf, and we get to know some of them quite well. Mama becomes good friends with Frau Battig, also from Stettin. This lady has a daughter, Renate, who is the same age as Gisela. A younger boy is in the family, too, and we girls don't mind when he wants to join in our games.

On Sundays, we usually go for walks together. City-bred Germans love to go for walks on a Sunday afternoon. The mothers lead the way. Though they appear deeply engrossed in conversation, they know exactly what we youngsters are up to at all times. Do they have eyes in the back?

"Don't climb up the embankment. You'll get your Sunday clothes dirty."

"No kicking stones. You'll ruin your good shoes."

"Watch where you're walking back there. You'll run into each other and get hurt."

Honestly, I wish we could be like the village kids and wear our old clothes on Sunday afternoons. It would be so nice to be allowed to run and climb and not to constantly worry about keeping our shoes and dresses perfectly clean. I know that Renate, the tomboy, would enjoy some more Sunday freedom, too.

Off and on, we visit a woman from Berlin, Frau Meisner, and her daughter, Brigitte, who is also as old as my sister. Frau Meisner serves us cake and makes polite conversation. Brigitte is a very nice girl, but a bit on the shy side. When she comes to visit us, she likes to play with our paper dolls. She is always quiet and extremely well mannered.

*

As winter approaches, Papa is due for another furlough. Happiness reigns. We will have him for two glorious weeks.

First on the agenda is a trip to Berlin, but only for him and for Mama. They are going to transport some of our belongings from the house in Rudow to Neuendorf. We are in desperate need of our warm clothing and linens and some other stuff. And while our parents are gone for two days, Gisela and I are allowed to go to Schössow's for dinner.

Meals in the restaurant should be a treat, but my sister and I feel rather uncomfortable without Mama's presence. The place happens to be filled with soldiers, and we have to sit in the midst of all those strangers in uniform. Gisela would rather crawl under the table than eat, I believe, but the men encourage her to take a bite, and then another, and another, until she is almost finished. Actually, they are very nice to us, but I still prefer not to linger longer than absolutely necessary.

It is so very good when I hear shuffling and familiar voices downstairs, and then my parents come through the door and up the stairs, safe and sound, lugging heavy suitcases and bundles. They have only been away for about thirty-six hours, but even this short period of time has felt like a small

167

eternity. Anything could've happened to them while in Berlin or on the train, and what would become of Gisela and me without them, far away from home? I don't think I've ever worried so much before in my life.

During the next few days, Papa helps us get ready for winter. He even saws wood for us and splits it into pieces. But … the pieces are too long and will not fit in the oven. Poor Papa!

Mama gets mad at him and scolds, "Can't you use your brain? Every chunk has to be shortened. Now we have all this extra work."

I feel so sorry for Papa.

The two weeks of being together as a complete family go by much too quickly. We would like to hold on to my father. He tells us to be brave. Then he's gone.

One Sunday evening, as my mother has tuned the radio to the station that broadcasts the weekly *Wunschkonzert*, a program that plays music requested by soldiers and dedicated to their loved ones back home, we hear, "And this one is sent to Wally, my dear wife, by Kurt Beetz." Then they play "*Heimat, deine Sterne*," which ends with the words "*ich liebe dich*."   When the song ends, Mama cries. We haven't seen her cry this hard in a long time. Gisela and I are also deeply touched.

Winter in our tiny apartment upstairs in Teetzens' house is cozy. We have enough wood to burn in the tile stove to keep us warm, and the small compartment above the fire chamber, at about face level for me, gets hot enough for making baked apples.

When it snows, we regret that we have no sleds — they are in Berlin, in the shed, but we can build snowmen and have snowball fights, and that's fun, too. And when big puddles of water in the meadow turn into shiny fields of ice, Gisela and I go sliding. We are allowed to do that, because some of our shoes have wooden soles. Wood doesn't get holes like leather. Isn't that lovely? Skates would come in handy here, but we have none.

Occasionally, we take a walk to the beach to observe the wintry sea. It looks cold and gray and forbidding. During a big cold spell, the water begins to freeze. Huge sheets of ice are forming, and the waves push them up and up and create mountains. This is truly a magnificent sight.

*

Nineteen forty-four is an interesting year, so much unlike all the previous ones. We are turning into true country folk, especially when Marie Teetzen puts us to work.

"Eva, take the cooked potato peels to the pigs. Will you do that for me?"

"Sure."

"Gisela, can you throw this food to the chickens?"

"Yes."

"The sheep have to be brought in. Can you go and get them?"

"Of course."

"Do you want to watch how I spin wool?"

"Oh, yes, certainly."

"Would you like to try it? Make sure you twirl the wool with your fingers to an even thickness."

"This isn't as easy as it looks."

During cherry picking time, we all pitch in. Teetzens have several trees in the garden, on the incline, where it goes up to Schössow's. They own more near their potato field, alongside the path that leads to the shortcut to Kolzow, the village where the butcher has his shop. When we pick cherries, Purzel usually accompanies us. The dog loves cherries as much as blueberries. Enough fall on the ground for her. If she swallows the pits or spits them out, I have no idea.

After all the picking is done and Frau Teetzen has washed the huge amount of cherries, she, my mother, Gisela, and I sit in a circle in the downstairs kitchen and remove the pits. Hours and hours it takes; our fingers turn red; our backs ache from bending over big pots and buckets. Moaning doesn't help. Marie Teetzen has no pity on us. Our reward is a big bowl of fresh cherries and, later, some jars of the canned fruit.

Then, one day, the butcher comes and slaughters one of the pigs. First, it has to hang from a hook at the corner of the house. I do not want to look at the dead animal, and I'm glad when it's finally taken down. After it is all cut up, our landlady puts some of the pieces into brine for curing, big hams are hung in the smoking chamber, and lots of meat goes into a grinder to be readied for sausage making.

"Frau Beetz, I could really use your help," says Frau Teetzen. "You can prepare a sausage mixture in this pot here in the kitchen, while I fix the other kind of sausage in the old kitchen. The spices are all on the table."

My mother looks into the big pot that's filled with a huge amount of ground, red, raw meat. She recoils.

"I've never mixed sausage before," she protests. "I don't know what to do."

"Sure you do. Just keep adding spices until it tastes something like salami. Nothing to it! I'll be back."

Frau Teetzen is out of the kitchen before we know it, and Gisela and I crowd around Mama to give her comfort and encouragement.

Salt, pepper, and various spices get thrown into the pot. Stir, stir, stir … Mama tastes the mixture. She shakes her head in disapproval. Some more of this, a bit more of that gets added. Again – stir, stir, and stir. Tasting follows. More spices are needed. And so it goes until, finally, a smile appears on Mama's face. She gives Gisela and me a sample. Indeed, it tastes like salami.

When Frau Teetzen comes to check up on the product, she seems pleased. "I knew you could do it," she says.

Mama beams.

Later, all the meat mixtures get stuffed into casings, tied at the ends, cooked, and then hung, as short and long sausages, into the smoking chamber where the hams have been placed shortly before.

A big celebration follows. Herr Teetzen's sisters-in-law, Martha and Lisbeth, are invited. They live on the adjoining properties, one to the right, and the other one to the left. And, of course, the big helpers, my mother, Gisela, and I are present, too.

The table is laden with pork roast and gravy and sausages, and with heaps of mashed potatoes and vegetables. What a feast! And when our bellies are really full and, under normal circumstances, shouldn't be able to hold more, our hostess brings out the most delicious cakes. Who can refuse?

"What should I do?" Gisela whines. "I'm stuffed, but I really want to taste some cake."

"Run around outside for a few minutes and then come back in," suggests Mama. "It will help settle the food. You'll see."

"Okay."

Off she goes, and we are amused as we watch Gisela run in the yard, back and forth and in circles.

A few minutes later, she's back, all smiles and ready for cake.

*

And then, one day, something exciting is happening. Our landlady announces she is going to take in a homeless child from the orphanage in Misdroy. Her own two sons have been fighting the war from the onset. One has been killed in action,

172

and the other one has not been heard from in quite some time. I assume Frau Teetzen's life feels kind of empty with none of her own children around. Or, perhaps, she's sorry for the kids who have no family to love them. So, one day, she sets out on her bicycle and comes home with the cutest little girl, about two years old, and then she proudly shows the new addition off to all her family and friends.

The little girl's name is Marianne. She has a round face with dimples; her eyes are big and dark brown, and her hair is almost black and has tight ringlets. Since her complexion is anything but fair, we wonder if she has Gypsy blood in her. But she is precious.

Marianne comes with barely any clothes. Frau Teetzen has cotton material, and Mama sews the most adorable outfits for the little girl.

After that, Mama has to also make dresses for Marie Teetzen. They happen to be winter dresses, but the woman can't wait for cold weather to arrive in order to let everybody see them, and so she wears them immediately, on hot days.

Mama stands by the window and laughs.

Very soon, bad news arrives. Little Marianne has to be returned to the orphanage. A relative has come forward to claim her. Frau Teetzen is sad.

But then, shortly after, another girl is offered to her. This one, apparently, is a child with absolutely no kin available or willing to raise her. She is already eight years old or so, her name is Waltraud, and she is blue-eyed and blond. She, too, is in great need of clothes.

"Frau Beetz, would you please sew some dresses for my Waltraud?" begs our landlady.

Mama, of course, cannot refuse. Again she spends hours at the sewing machine.

Waltraud is put to work in the kitchen. When she washes dishes, water splashes all over her nice, new dresses. This is not good. My mother has to sew aprons.

*

I'm in seventh grade by now. A few high school books have arrived from Berlin, and I have to study them.

Frau Professor Michel still gives me English lessons, and my mother has found a retired math teacher who is willing to instruct me in algebra. I have some catching up to do, and this man knows how to make me race through the material, page after page, and chapter after chapter. He's lucky I have a good mind for numbers.

In the meantime, I'm elected to teach English to Gisela and her friends, Renate and Brigitte. Gisela is a better learner than the other girls.

In our little country school, we have an eighth grader who already looks quite womanly – tall and very rounded. When the teacher goes over adjectives, this big girl has no idea what he is talking about. She cannot give a single example.

With a rather disdainful look, he names some. "Fat, dumb, stupid, lazy, gluttonous." I don't think the girl realizes that he is describing her. She's just an overgrown, somewhat klutzy country bumpkin with a small brain. She probably has to help a lot on the farm, and nobody in her family places much value on book learning.

A boy by the name of Klaus Gurgel, evacuee from Berlin, often comes around and asks, "Do you want to come down and play?"

It's entertaining to spend time with him. We often go into the nearby woods and play cowboys and Indians. Shooting with homemade bows and arrows is great fun. All we need for that are a few supple branches, a bit of string, and some thin, straight sticks. Sometimes, we play hide and seek, or we simply race up and down the embankments, with or without gleeful noise.

Gisela thinks Klaus has a crush on me, but I don't believe it. He's only eleven or twelve years old, much too young to have a crush on anybody. I'm already twelve, and I don't have a romantic bone in my body.

We have sports in school, anything we can do in our schoolyard. When we play *Völkerball*, dodge ball, I hope the ball doesn't come in my direction. It's such a hard ball, and it hurts a lot when it hits the stomach or the chest. But I stand my ground, when necessary, and catch that awful ball. I would never want my team to lose because of my cowardice.

I'm still a good runner and jumper, and I'm great at doing chin-ups. Therefore, when news is delivered about a sports competition from the Usedom/Wollin school district, two or three of us from Neuendorf are being taken to a stadium in the big town, Swinemünde, I believe, and we try our best to win. We receive no medals. True athletes would have gone through rigorous training before a competition. What do we have? Some laps around the schoolyard and a few jumps into a dirt pile.

For swim lessons, we go to the lake behind the school. But the only possible way into the water is from the other side, and so we have to walk halfway around the lake to that open spot first. Honestly, the lake is not the cleanest body of water. It is muddy, has green duckweed covering large areas, and an overabundance of nasty plant growth. It is understandable, though, that our teacher rather takes us to the lake than to the sea, for safety reasons. Also, it's a lot closer.

Those kids, who, by the end of the series of lessons, are able to swim – no touching the ground – for fifteen minutes, receive a *Freischwimmer* certificate. Gisela is among them. She probably could've managed the forty-five minute test, but she gets badly tangled in seaweed and has to fight her way out of the mess. I, too, struggle with the underwater jungle, but I come free again. My certificate makes me a *Fahrtenschwimmer*, one who can swim long distance. I feel bad for Gisela, because she, the water rat, is the better swimmer by far.

During summer vacation, all pupils have to take turns caring for silkworms that have been placed in our school building, in trays, on long tables. We have to feed grape leaves to those ugly things. It is very generous of the mayor to let us pick leaves from his many grapevines.

"We have to help our troops," says the teacher. "They need the silk for parachutes."

The troops probably need more than silk spun by our worms. They could use some extra fighting power. Allied forces have invaded France, landing on the coast of Normandy. They are driving our soldiers back. But … we have the newly developed V-1 bomb, which we are going to launch against England. And the V-2 bomb is coming. Surely, those bombs will get things turned around. Just wait and see.

*

Marie Teetzen has a big job lined up for us again. This time, it's making syrup from sugar beets. She and her husband have dug them up from their field, enormous amounts of them, and she has scrubbed them clean and cooked them in enormous kettles. After mashing them, she has squeezed the juice out with some wooden contraption. Now the sweet liquid has to be boiled down until it is syrup. Two huge pots of juice stand near the water pump. One pot is carried to the kitchen in the big house; the other one will be taken care of in the kitchen of the old house.

"Frau Beetz, you may stir this pot here until I come back." She leaves my mother in the main kitchen, while she takes Gisela and me to the other kitchen.

"And you two can be in charge of this pot. You have to keep on stirring, the whole bottom, not just in the center or only around the sides. If you don't do it right, it will burn. Then the syrup is ruined. Do you understand?"

"Yes."

"I'll be back in a while to take over."

So Gisela and I take turns stirring, and we don't dare to stop, not even for a few seconds. We do not want the syrup to get ruined. It is a very monotonous, tiring job.

An eternity later, Frau Teetzen returns to the kitchen to make sure everything is all right. "Keep on stirring," she reminds us. "You're doing a good job. I'll be back later." Then she is gone again.

The juice begins to thicken. Now we have to be even more careful. The thicker the juice, the easier it burns. I feel somewhat uneasy.

"It's coming along. Keep on stirring. I'll be back," says Frau Teetzen.

Her visits become more frequent now.

Eventually, the syrup is dark golden brown and has the right consistency. Now Frau Teetzen moves the heavy pot aside. She ladles off the foam and tells us, "This is delicious on bread. You'll love it. And, of course, you'll enjoy the syrup, too."

Finally, we are released from our kitchen duty. When we check up on Mama, she's still stirring her syrup, but it is also ready to be taken off the burner.

178

Later, we ask, "Mama, did Frau Teetzen help you with the syrup?"

"No, she only came in to check, off and on. I thought she was with you two."

"No."

"I guess she had other things to do."

In appreciation of our help, Marie Teetzen presents us with a big bowl of delicious syrup and a small dish of the foam. Really, the foam tastes yummy on bread.

When potato-digging time comes around, my mother helps in the field. All able-bodied grownups and many children are doing fieldwork. There just aren't enough men around for the job, and so even the city women have to do their share to bring in the harvest. Gisela and I spend only a short time gathering potatoes into baskets. Otherwise, we stay in the apartment and take care of the housework.

*

Our V-1 attacks don't seem to be successful. Honestly, the situation doesn't look good at all. The Americans are advancing. Toward the end of September, the *Volkssturm* is put into existence. All German men between the ages of sixteen and sixty have to report for duty. That's still-wet-behind-the-ears boys and old men! The youngsters have no training. They don't know how to fight.

Then comes a big, important announcement that every boy and girl of Hitler Youth age, with no exception, has to show up at a meeting in Kolzow. In other words, all kids ten and older. "There will be no ration cards for those who don't show up," we are told.

So, on the specified day, we all troop to the neighboring village, using the shortcut through the woods. Nobody owns a uniform.

We meet in a church. Our names are taken down. Young adults – in uniform – make a few speeches. We sing patriotic songs, of which one of them is, of course, *"Deutschland, Deutschland über alles, über alles in der Welt." Sieg Heils* are shouted, too, and then we are dismissed. Now we have done our duty and are entitled to our ration cards. What a relief!

Even in Neuendorf we have bomb alarms. When this happens, we take shelter in Teetzens' cold storage cellar, a dugout that has a nice dirt cover on top, because it is built into a little hill. Of course, if a bomb should fall on or near this shelter, the whole thing would cave in immediately.

When enemy planes are not directly overhead, we stand outside, by the door, and look toward Stettin, the usual site of the bombings. What a spectacle! Searchlights cross the night sky. Flares shoot up like fireworks. They remain in the air for a while, giving the illusion of candles on a Christmas tree. And then … the sky turns red. Stettin is burning. How many people have lost their homes, and perhaps their lives, this time?

Once, a bomb falls a few miles away. It destroys the restaurant by a lake, a favorite tourist destination.

We fear for Oma's and Opa's safety, and we are always relieved when a letter arrives from Berlin. Papa still writes regularly, but his missives don't always make it to us as fast as they should.   When we have to wait too long, Mama panics.

*

Winter begins. Icy winds blow, especially by the Baltic Sea. We, the school children are led to the snow-covered dunes where the thorny, willow-leafed sea blackthorn bushes grow that have orange berries, loaded with vitamin C.

"We have to pick as many of these *Sanddornbeeren* as we can," we are told. "They are being used for the manufacturing of vitamin tablets. Our soldiers need them."

So we pick lots and lots of these tiny, clustered berries, and the wind stings our faces, and our hands get so cold they hurt. We have to do our duty. If the vitamin tablets, if actually made, ever get to the soldiers, is questionable.

Nobody in his sane mind believes in a German victory anymore. Everybody is worried. But the Nazis, they are shivering in their shoes. Who knows what the Russians are going to do with them when they get to us. Yes, we are already convinced the enemy from the East will advance all the way to

Neuendorf and farther. Unless, of course, the Americans, who are coming closer and closer to Germany, hurry up and make it to us first.

New Year's Eve we celebrate with the Battigs. We have a kind of come-what-may-and-let's-be-happy-today attitude. Mama sacrifices the bottle of champagne, which Papa has brought with him from France, on his last visit.

"We intended to drink it together, when Kurt comes home after the war," she says before popping the cork, "but I think we better finish it now. Who knows what will happen later."

Even my sister and I and the Battig kids get some of the sparkling wine. I think it tastes pretty good.

Glasses in hand, at the stroke of midnight, we stand by the open window and shout, *"Prost Neujahr!"* Either Frau Battig or my mother makes the remark, "I wonder how the mayor feels at this moment." Then the other one answers, "Not very happy, I'm sure. He's probably scared stiff. He's the biggest Nazi around. Just wait and see, he'll go into hiding soon."

The Battigs have a small second-floor apartment in a house that sits up on an incline. From their window, we can see the mayor's big, beautiful house below. No sounds of merry-making are coming from there.

*

For less than a month, we live in eerie suspension. Then come the seemingly endless streams of refugees and the retreating soldiers, events that bring the ugliness of war into close-up view and cause an increasing fear of the unknown.

How much time will we have before the enemy arrives? What fate awaits us? Nobody can give us an answer. We just know that the Russians are moving closer and closer.

Mail service is suspended. Our school remains closed. Our teacher is gone from Neuendorf. My English tutor, Frau Professor Michel, and her husband have left for Hannover. Where my math tutor has disappeared to, we have no idea. At least, the Michels have said good-bye to us and offered us to go along with them, but my wonderful algebra helper has taken off without a word.

People dig holes and hide their valuables in the ground. Mama buries a suitcase with linens and stuff.

Despite the general unease, we are going to celebrate Easter, which falls on April l this year, four days before my thirteenth birthday. Oh, it's a bright, warm day, and we will have an Easter egg hunt in the woods. The Battigs are going to join us.

"You shouldn't go into the woods," says Marie Teetzen. "Somebody has spotted a naked black roaming there." She sounds serious.

My mother bursts out laughing. "Where is he supposed to have come from? And why would he be naked? What an imagination!"

Frau Teetzen shrugs. Undoubtedly, she has never seen a real black man before. And come to think of it, neither have I, except in illustrations and in a Shirley Temple movie.

So, all dressed up in our Sunday best, we stroll into the woods until we come to a sun-bathed clearing. Mama makes us sit on the trunk of a fallen tree, and we are not allowed to peek while she is hiding the egg-shaped cookies, which she has baked the day before and then carefully wrapped in pieces of paper. As soon as she gives the signal, we fan out and begin our hunt.

"This is fun!" exclaims Frau Battig. "What ever gave you the idea of baking Easter eggs? This is absolutely marvelous."

"We have to have something for the kids," says my mother. "Plain cookie dough was the only thing I could come up with. I didn't even have an egg to mix in."

Our few Easter treasures are devoured in no time at all, and then we four children play games while the mothers sit and talk. Oh, we are having a carefree time.

*

A few days later, the dreaded news spreads like wildfire through the village. "The Russian are coming. They are only a few kilometers away."

With fear, we watch the road from Warnow. There! The first soldiers come into view.

184

"Quickly, hide in the cellar," says Frau Teetzen. She opens the little trapdoor in the hallway and pushes us down the ladder. Then she shoves Frau Gurgel and Klaus, her son, who have recently moved into Teetzens' little, old house, where we have cooked syrup not long ago, in with us. The door gets slammed shut, and then we hear thumping and scraping above, as our landlady pushes a big chest over the trapdoor.

It is a tiny storage cellar, even smaller than Tante Lotte's, and it has only a very small vent hole to the outside and no light. We are five people down there, and my mother is claustrophobic. In her anxiety, she has trouble breathing. She squirms, throws her arms up, and she wants to scream. The other woman holds her down and whispers, "Quiet. They will hear us. They will find us."

Eventually, heavy footsteps can be heard upstairs. Loud, strange voices, in a foreign tongue, make us shiver with fear. The soldiers, apparently, are searching the house. Now they stomp through the hallway, above the cellar. What, if they detect the trapdoor? We do not move. We hardly dare to breathe.

How long Frau Teetzen keeps us hidden in our dark cell, I cannot recall. But when we finally climb out and inhale fresh air, it feels good.

"I don't think they will come back today. Go upstairs, get something to eat, and sleep." And then she adds, "I'll barricade the doors down here so no soldiers can barge right in."

185

As we walk up the stairs, we can hear Marie Teetzen move furniture.

Yes, we are tired, exhausted from the frightening hours in the tight quarters below, and very hungry. When my mother opens the cupboard, she immediately notices that things are missing. Our big salami is gone, the one she has been saving for our eventual flight to a safer location. A few other items have disappeared, too, but that stolen salami is what upsets Mama the most. She is really mad.

The next few days are truly awful. When house searches seem imminent, we disappear into the hole, and our landlady slides the chest into place. As soon as the coast is clear, we come out again. Frau Teetzen considers herself too old to be in danger. "The Russians are looking for young females to molest," she says.

Then, one day, hiding is out of the question. Everybody is ordered out of the village. Like the refugees and the soldiers, a few weeks ago, we have to march out of Neuendorf, but in the opposite direction, and we have no wagons or wheelbarrows; we only take along what we can carry in our hands.

"Where are they taking us?"

"What are they going to do with us?"

"What's going to happen?"

"No idea. It doesn't look good."

So we walk down the road and worry.

Suddenly, Mama asks, "Gisela, Evchen, should we try to disappear into the woods and make our way to the sea?"

"And then what?" I cannot imagine what she has in mind.

"Walk into the Baltic and drown ourselves."

"Why?"

"It may be better than getting shot or taken to Siberia."

I remember the drowning victim, a woman, washed up on the beach a few weeks ago. I cannot get the sight of her bloated body out of my mind. No, I don't want to end up like her. I rather take my chances with the Russians.

"My answer is no," I say.

"And I'm not going to drown myself, either," declares Gisela.

Mama says no more.

When we get to Kolzow, we are allowed to stop. We still have no idea what this is all about.

Hours later, we are told to go home again.

Neuendorf has not been burned to the ground. That's a relief. But a lot of plundering has taken place during our absence.

"Not everyone made the trek to Kolzow," people whisper. "Some suddenly-turned Communists stayed behind, and you know who they are. Those connivers switched allegiance to be on the Russians' good side, and they most likely took part in the looting. They are nothing but hoodlums."

Soon after, we are chased out of Neuendorf again. This time, we have to take the road to Warnow. Everyone looks bedraggled, especially the women. They wear scarves on their heads, pulled down low to hide their soot-smeared faces. Nobody wants to appear young and desirable and become a rape victim.

We tote as many possessions as we can, for we don't know how long we will be on this march, or if we will ever return to Neuendorf. Gisela has been given a pot to carry, which has a few utensils in it.

"It's too heavy," she complains. "My arms hurt."

"Come on now," says Mama. "Your stuff weighs barely anything. Stop whining."

We only have to go as far as Warnow, which, under normal circumstances, can be reached in one hour. Since nobody is in a hurry, we trot slowly. Sympathetic families take us in, for which we are very grateful. When night falls, they offer us some beds. Placing ourselves like sardines in a can, we fit at least ten people on each bed. Others rest on the floor. If someone has to get out, it's extremely difficult to make it to the door without stepping on a sleeper. It's even harder to get your place back upon return.

Next morning, the shout can be heard, "Everybody out! We're going home."

Back in our village again, we find holes in the yard. A hole poked here, a hole there, and there, and everywhere, as if chipmunks have come for an invasion. Other places are dug up. Of course, the hidden treasures have been found and taken away. Gone are Mama's linens in the suitcase.

One afternoon soon after, a certain number of young women and girls are being herded up to the big house on the hill. We have no inkling what this is about. When we hear screams coming from somewhere in the building, the women in our room have a pretty good idea of what the Russian soldiers have in mind for their amusement.

"Does the window open?"

"Yes."

"Any soldiers in sight?"

"No."

"Let's get out of here."

It's easier said then done, because, just then, one of the Russians comes into the room and motions the children to leave the house. He goes out, too, and disappears from our view.

As Gisela and I round the corner, we see Mama by the window. She's the first one to climb out. Together, we sneak away in silence, trying to stay behind bushes. When we come to the embankment, we crawl and slide down. Then we race down the lane. As soon as we get to the house, panting, we make Frau Teetzen hide us.

This is scary. *Have the soldiers seen our escape? Are they following us? Will they find us?*

We cower in darkness. We make no sound. We listen.

No banging door. No heavy footsteps. No angry Russian voices.

Frau Teetzen eventually releases us from our prison.

One day, a soldier surprises us upstairs, in our apartment. He looks around; then he drags my struggling mother into the small storage room next to our bedroom. Gisela and I stand back in horror. As soon as we get over the initial, paralyzing fear, we follow the two. I push the curtain that covers the entrance to the narrow, cramped-full-with-stuff room aside, and I see the man pressed against my mother. She looks so very scared.

He has no right to do that. I have to protect her. How?

"Let go of my mother!" I scream.

"Go! Get out of here! Go downstairs! Both of you! Now!" Oh, Mama sounds frantic. And so we run down the stairs as fast as our legs can take us and stay with Frau Teetzen until the bad man is out of the house.

Mama does not tell us what has happened.

*

As time goes by, a relative calm settles over Neuendorf. Order is being restored. No more harassment, rapes, raids. Some of the Russian soldiers actually try to make friends with the German people. We begin to see them not as beasts but as decent human beings. Oh, yes, there are a few goof balls and ignoramuses among them, but which nation doesn't have them?

To mind comes the soldier who picks up our alarm clock. It rings. He throws it out the window and shoots it. I also think of the soldier who "borrows" Marie Teetzen's bicycle, tries to ride it but doesn't know how. He falls a few times, gets mad at the thing … and punishes it by putting a few bullets in it. Bello, our little canine friend, who dares to bark, gets shot, too.

One friendly Russian, speaking German, occasionally stops to talk to us over the fence. He tells us he's a shoemaker by trade and has a good wife and several children back home. Off and on, he brings milk for Gisela and me.

All grownups have to go to work. The commandant orders, "This group works in the field. You all sweep the streets. You do this job, and you do that." Only the laborers are allowed to line up for food. I do not know who takes care of the old and the sick.

My mother mostly works in one of the mansions the officers have taken over. She helps in the kitchen. Some of the Russians are very nice, she reports. One, who calls himself Kolle – she thinks it probably stands for Karl, sometimes puts hard candy and marzipan in her apron pocket to take home to her children. Of course, we are delighted to receive treats.

"Kolle is refined," Mama says. "But some of the ordinary soldiers who work for the officers must have rather uncivilized backgrounds. They use the coat closet as bathroom; in the toilet bowl, they wash the potatoes."

While Mama is working, Gisela and I are responsible for our little household. We clean and cook. When Mama comes home on her lunch break, a meal is waiting for her.

Something strange is going on when we are doing the dishes, and it happens with regularity. I wash, Gisela dries. As soon as I begin to scrub the first pot, I have to take off for the outhouse. It's an emergency. Honestly.

"Finish washing the pots, Gisela," I say and run.

"You do this on purpose!" she screams.

"No, I don't!" I holler back, already halfway down the stairs.

We don't mind doing the housework. It's something that gives us a purpose. The school is still closed, and we don't even open our textbooks to study the last pages on our own. Who wants to think of an education when life is in shambles?

Then, one day in May, rumor gets to us that the fighting is over. Germany has lost the war. What now?

CHAPTER FOUR

THE AFTERMATH

Spring turns into summer. We have no radio connection, no newspaper, and no mail deliveries. Off and on, someone reports bits and pieces of what is going on outside of Neuendorf.

"Train service has been restored ... to a certain extent. Lots of people are returning to the cities they've come from. Yes, there are trains leaving from Warnow."

Hearing the news, Mama decides it is time for us to pack up and go back to Berlin. We have no idea what we will find when we get there.

We will carry as much clothing on our bodies as we can tolerate. So we dress in layers – multiple sets of underwear, several dresses, sweater, and coat. We certainly look well rounded, and we are hot. Everyone has to carry as much as possible, even Gisela.

My sister and I are allowed to take along one toy. Should we take our dolls? They are ready for the journey, dressed in layers of clothing, like Gisela and I, their mothers. No, we decide to leave the dolls behind and carry our pet rabbit instead.

"Are you sure you want to bother with Mucki? He might present a problem."

"Of course, Mucki has to come with us. We can't leave him here."

My mother shakes her head, but then she fastens a handle to a box and Mucki gets shoved into his container. I have to lug the uncomfortable load plus my other stuff.

After saying good-bye to the Teetzens, we set out for Warnow, on foot. Dressed the way we are, and with heavy luggage in our hands and on our backs, it takes us much longer than normal to get to the railroad station. Once on the platform, we patiently wait for a train to arrive. There is no set schedule.

When we finally board, we are lucky to find a space on a freight car. We sit on the floor; our assortment of luggage is piled around us. The rabbit is allowed to stick his head out of the box, on occasion. Other travelers look on and strike up conversations. At an unscheduled stop, Mucki escapes and hides under the train. I cannot recall how many fellow passengers join in the rescue effort. After this frightful episode, I'm very careful our pet causes no more excitement.

In certain places, the tracks are damaged. Then we have to get out of the freight car, walk a while, and board another train. Each time, we fear no room will be left for us, in which case we would have to wait who knows how long for the next opportunity to get to Berlin.

Eventually, we arrive in our city. We are exhausted. We are also appalled by the destruction we come to witness.

How fortunate! Public transportation is still available … or again.

We head for Britz, and we find my grandparents' apartment building undamaged.

With a new burst of energy, we climb the stairs to the second floor. Mama rings the doorbell. We notice someone peeking through the little spy hole. The door flings open ... we are in my grandmother's arms.

Opa, apparently having heard the commotion, comes down the long hallway, half walking, half running, and joins in the happy reunion. Then he helps us carry our ragtag belongings into the apartment. Mucki gets put on the balcony, where he, finally free, delights in hopping around like a little beast high on pep pills.

Mama, Gisela, and I remove our excess clothing, clean up a bit, and then sit down with my grandparents to get a bite to eat and exchange the most important news.

"You can't go back to live in the house in Rudow," Oma informs us. "It's damaged too much. It's not safe."

"Then where should we go?"

"Stay here. We'll manage somehow."

"Do you know that Berlin has been divided into four sectors? The Russians, the French, the British, and the Americans each took a part."

"And where are we?"

"In the American sector."

"Any word from the men yet?"

"No."

After some deliberation, Opa's bed gets moved into the living room. Gisela will bunk with Oma on the *chaiselongue.* Mama and I have Oma's bed to share. For my grandparents, I'm sure it must be an unnerving situation. We, the returnees to Berlin, are used to total confusion by now, and, really, having a roof over our heads is all that matters at the moment.

*

We are subject to registration in Britz. For that, Mama must go to the police station. Under normal circumstances, when people move, they have to properly notify the authorities that they are leaving the area. They then present their signed document to the clerk in charge at the new location. With no official in the village of Neuendorf available, we have not been able to observe this rule. Apparently, the Britz registrar is used to such negligence from many people returning to the city. Normalcy, in times of chaos, goes out the window.

Where do Berliners live, whose apartments and houses have been turned into rubble? If they have no relatives or friends to take them in, they make their homes in basements, bunkers, and refugee camps. We are so lucky; we have found a haven in Oma's and Opa's apartment.

Once the formality of registration is out of the way, Mama, Gisela, and I walk to Rudow. We have to inspect our house. To our delight, we find it in good enough condition to enter without being afraid the roof might fall on us. Some of our belongings can be salvaged. On that first trip, we take to Britz what we can carry. For subsequent hauls, we use a little wagon. A few chairs, some pots and pans and dishes, and the old crib are among the items being pulled through the streets.

We salvage our two adult beds, which, when pushed together, make a double bed, German style. Mama and I sleep in them. Gisela will have to make do with the crib, which my ingenious mother extends with a few boards. Unfortunately, the boards, a bit too short, don't stay in place, and they regularly hit the floor with a great clatter. Poor Gisela!

Since the legs of our table are still usable, but the top is ruined, Mama fashions a new tabletop from the solid headboards of our beds. "I never liked them, anyhow," she says. "Now they are good for something."

Eventually, we acquire a wardrobe and a small closet. Getting settled takes time and a lot of effort.

Oma's and Opa's former bedroom is now our domain, but as soon as it gets really cold, it's ours only during the night. The big, beautiful tile oven in what used to be my grandparent's living room doesn't work anymore, and so Opa huddles in our room, with his back to the oven, for as long as a fire gives off some warmth during the day. Oma prefers to sit in the kitchen, most of the time.

Oh, yes, we also bring Mama's Singer sewing machine to Britz, and this is very important, because

Mama finds a job sewing blouses from silky, gray, wartime parachute material. She picks up the bundles of already cut cloth, and then she takes the finished blouses back to the lady who runs the business from her home in Rudow. The pay is lousy. But sewing flimsy blouses is still better than working on the bucket brigade with the army of women who, because men are not available, sort and remove the bricks from the many ruins. Anything that looks reusable gets the mortar knocked off, and the cleaned blocks, in buckets, then make their way, from woman to woman, to the piles near the road. Yes, the women are in charge of cleaning up the war-damaged city.

Opa, retired by now, spends many hours sitting in his chair, reading the newspaper, which he receives free, because he has worked for the paper for so many years. Or he plays cards with an invisible opponent. He also walks to the park where, in good weather, a group of old men sit on the benches and wile away the hours, talking.

Oma, Gisela, and I try to secure fuel. Every day, we search the streets for broken branches and any debris that can be burned. We even pick up tarpaper, which, we know quite well, causes heavy smoke and ruins the chimney. Since we are desperate, we don't care about the consequences.

The stores have little to sell. They only receive wares according to what is allotted to the people, which is 800 calories per person, a bit more for workers doing heavy jobs ... and only 600 calories for children. Men are lucky, for they receive ration stamps for cigarettes. If they curtail their smoking, they can trade their cigarettes for food on the black market.

Tante Dora and Tante Käthe have both returned to Berlin. Tante Käthe first works on the bucket brigade, but then she lands a job with NCR (National Cash Register); Tante Dora is in her old hospital position. The two sisters share an apartment.

Mama and Tante Käthe make two trips to Neuendorf. On the first one, they bring back our belongings, but the second one is for the purpose of picking up bags of potatoes, promised to them by Marie Teetzen. Though quite a few potatoes are already gray and blue and somewhat rotten from age, we think they are a gift from heaven.

*

Life, however downgraded, has to return to somewhat normal. And so, Gisela and I get registered for school. Mama is furious when the director of the *Britzer Dorfschule* suggests I should be put back a year because of my missed high school education while in Neuendorf.

"Eva had her books for home study, and she took English and algebra lessons from tutors," she fumes. "I insist you put her in the class she belongs. You have no right to hold her back."

My mother wins.

Under normal circumstances, Gisela would belong in high school, second grade, but she has missed the entire first year of classes. Many youngsters are in the same situation due to their evacuation. For the time being, Gisela starts out in the elementary school next to the firehouse, practically across from our apartment building. Not much later, a special high school class is being created for students like my sister, who have to catch up on the missed academic subjects.

We have no textbooks. Paper is scarce. We take notes of everything the instructors try to teach us. I write extremely small, even between the lines. Only tests deserve normal spacing, because, otherwise, the teachers wouldn't be able to decipher my tiny scribbles.

French is the new subject now. I love it. It's almost as much fun as English. Only the girls have French; the boys, now in a separate classroom, have to learn Latin. They hate it.

After a while, it is decreed that boys and girls should be coeducated. The boys hate that, too. They want nothing to do with the girls. They pretend we females don't exist. The ill feeling between the sexes is upsetting, and we girls decide something has to be done about it. We demand a meeting.

Trying to look very macho, the boys take their stand in the corner of the schoolyard.

The girls cluster around a bench not too far away.

"What do you want?" asks the toughest one of the male bunch.

"We want to be treated in a decent way," says our girl speaker.

"Why?"

"Because it's very unpleasant to sit in the same room with you guys when you ignore us or give us dirty looks. We should really try to get along."

After some huddling and a lot of feet shuffling, the boys promise, on a trial basis, to be courteous to the girls.

Though the open hostility makes way to tolerance, friendliness is still a long way off.

Since the forced integration, we are seated in alphabetical order. I'm in the front row, third seat in. Sharing a bench with me is a tall, dark, rather handsome young fellow, whose last name also starts with a B. He tries to position himself so he doesn't have to see me … until, one day, when we have a test, and he doesn't know the answer to a question. Suddenly, though I'm a girl, I seem to be worthy of a nudge, a pleading look, and a secret pointing at my paper. I even earn a grateful smile for letting him glance at my solution. From that day on, he treats me like a friendly neighbor. Slowly, the other boys let down their guard, too, and we all coexist in a somewhat amiable way.

*

One day in late fall, but I don't remember exactly when, we hear a knock at the door. My mother leaves the kitchen to see who might be calling on us.

201

Moments later, we are startled by her scream. Gisela and I rush to the hallway to see what has happened.

We find Mama leaning against the wall, looking like a wounded animal.

"What's the matter?" we call as we rush toward her.

"They say Papa is dead," she answers in a weak voice.

"Who says?" I ask.

"The two men who brought the telegram."

"Let me see it."

I take the piece of paper from her hand.

Sure enough, the message states that Kurt Beetz has been killed in action on March 22, 1945, in Landau, the Rhineland Palatinate.

"They've made a mistake." My mother shakes her head with vigor. "Papa isn't dead. He can't be. I would've known. No, no. It's not true. They've got the wrong person. You'll see."

Then she breaks down and cries. Gisela howls. I lead both into the bedroom. By now, I'm so concerned about the two that, though I'm deeply saddened myself, I'm unable to shed tears. Somehow, I feel as if I have to be strong and in control. Yes, my father would want it this way. I cannot let him down.

When Oma and Opa are told the news, they take it calmly. It is possible they have a private conversation with my mother later, but I'm not around to witness it.

The next day, Mama takes Gisela and me aside, and she says, "Don't tell anyone about the telegram. Remember, not a single person has to know about it."

"Why?" we want to know.

"Because children without a father are looked down upon. And, besides, Papa isn't dead. He'll come home. Just wait and see."

So we promise not to tell. I feel very uncomfortable about the situation. Now I have to lie to my friends and even to the relatives. It's awful. Sometimes, I don't know what my mother is thinking. If she would only accept reality!

*

Onkel Gerhard, Tante Gertrud, and their little daughter, Christa, return to Berlin. They have a house and a nice garden in Britz, near the Teltow Canal, about fifteen minutes away from us. Oh, Onkel Gerhard has been the lucky one. Taken prisoner and held in a lightly guarded detention camp in the West for a while, he has been able to escape and make his way to his in-laws' farm in Landeck. We learn that he has been seriously ill en route, supposedly from sleeping on the cold, wet ground of the forest. This has given him rheumatic fever and a damaged heart. But, at least, he's still alive, and his family can be happy.

We like having Onkel Gerhard around again, especially when he laughs and plays his accordion. A bit of music is good for the soul.

Tante Gertrud goes to work in the afternoons and on Saturdays. My uncle has a job, too. Who has to baby-sit just-about-two-year-old Christa? Gisela and I are given this job – without being asked first. We are not very happy about this arrangement. We do not like to care for a difficult, spoiled, misbehaving toddler. It is revolting to see the little one crumble her bread and throw it on the floor. And when she drinks her milk, she lets it dribble down her chin and onto the table. Of course, she is only a tiny kid and hasn't learned yet how to eat with manners, but it rips my heart to watch the waste. We never have enough to satisfy our bellies, and hunger hurts.

Christa is privileged; she is entitled to a milk ration, a luxury reserved for the very young. She also has enough bread to eat, because Onkel Gerhard drives a bread truck and gets his hands on extra loaves. He never gives us a few slices, not even for watching his daughter all the time.

"I forgive him for not sharing with us, but he should at least slip some to Oma and Opa, his hungry parents." Mama gets angry off and on, but she does not say anything to her brother. I guess she wants to keep the peace.

In bad times, people often forget to be compassionate. They only look out for themselves.

Since not much food can be had in the stores, the black market flourishes. But in order to obtain goods, you have to have something of value to trade. We are poor. Our few treasures have disappeared during the war, and Mama doesn't even receive a monthly allotment of cigarettes, because she is a woman. Cigarettes can get you many things. Some people are so hooked on them they rather do without food than without a glimmer stick between their lips.

The few functioning trains that run between the city and the outlying areas, all situated in the Russian zone, are always jam-packed with hungry Berliners trying to trade with the farmers, who are now the wealthy ones, because they own the crops and the livestock. The farmers have become very choosy. They only accept the best goods for a bit of flour, some potatoes, or a few turnips.

"They are so rich now," say the city dwellers, "they can put rugs in the pig pens."

Mama makes a few grueling train trips to the East Zone herself, and I don't know what she trades, but she always returns very tired and saddened. Every tiny bit of food she unpacks makes Gisela and me happy.

Once, my mother takes me along. Now I realize why she is so very disheartened. Like beggars, we go from door to door. Often, nobody answers when we knock. Other times, the farmer's wife opens her door just a crack, takes a peek at what Mama has to offer, and then she shakes her head and sends us away.

Finally, a young woman agrees to give us a bag of split peas for the embroidered tablecloth my mother has shown her. She seems pleased with the swap. We look forward to having soup.

"Now let's hurry," says my mother. "We don't want to miss the next train."

With the bag of peas carefully hidden under her coat, she drags me through the village. She eyes every Russian soldier with suspicion, and she is especially nervous when we have to pass the guards at the railroad station.

"Sometimes, they confiscate food stuff," she whispers to me.

Oh, no, they better not take our peas, I think. Now I'm nervous, too.

Soon we can hear the train in the distance. When it comes into view, we are not sure, if we will be able to board it, for we see passengers on the running boards, the buffers, and on top of the roofs. We are fortunate. Some compassionate men get out of the way, push us into the safety of the car, and then they take up their places on the running board again.

Mama thanks them, and I'm afraid they might lose their grip and fall off the train.

I am so glad when this whole adventure is over.

We share the few peas with my grandparents, but when Tante Gertrud finds out about our "good fortune," she is jealous.

*

Winter arrives. It is cold, everywhere. The apartment is cold; the classrooms are cold. We bundle up as much as we can, and we even wear our coats indoors. Whatever pieces of wood we come across in the streets, in the parks, and in the rubble, we burn in the kitchen stove.

It has become impossible to find grass for Mucki now, and so the rabbit has to make do with dried leaves. In his desperation for real food, he snitches a potato.

"Mucki has a potato!" Gisela suddenly yells.

A valuable potato gone! We have to get it back!

In a flash, I'm in the kitchen. Oma jumps off her chair. We join Gisela in the effort to corner the rabbit.

Mucki runs from the kitchen into the living room, the potato clenched between his teeth. Around and around the table he hops, and we three humans are in hot pursuit. We win. The potato is ours. Poor rabbit. He would have enjoyed the feast.

A few weeks later, Mucki is near death. We call one of the neighbors for help. He puts our pet out of his misery, removes his innards and skins him. We have rabbit stew.

Mama gets very sick with the flu. Her fever is quite high, and she has to stay in bed. Then Gisela comes down with the same illness, and my grandmother and I have two patients on our hands. Oma watches them while I'm in school. When I get home, I take over. A few days later, I, too, am feverish and aching all over. I would love to crawl

207

into bed like the others, but I feel obligated to keep on going.

During one of my blue days, when I feel as if the weight of the world rests upon my shoulders, the teacher happens to talk about death. How she gets to this subject, I cannot recall.

She asks, "Who has never been to a funeral?"

A few hands go up, and mine is one of them.

"Oh, you are so lucky. None of your family members or friends has died."

"How can you dare to make such a statement?" I feel like screaming. "My father is dead, killed in the war. Who knows what has become of Onkel Willi? He's probably buried somewhere in Russia." I'm very, very angry, but I'm not allowed to speak up. Mama still doesn't want anybody to know about Papa.

*

It is nice to live with my grandparents. Oma teaches us all kinds of funny songs. Since we have been without a radio since the Russians have confiscated ours in Neuendorf, and Oma and Opa have never owned one, to the best of my knowledge, we don't hear transmitted music anymore. This is sad, but we are so occupied with our daily hardships that we don't even think about what we used to enjoy. Honestly, 1945 has not been a year for song and laughter.

Mama has taken on some clients. They come to the house to get measured and fitted. Though they seem genuinely pleased with their new dresses, they pay only a pittance. Some customers want an old garment altered, or they expect my mother to work miracles and create a beautiful, new dress out of someone else's discarded piece of clothing. My mother works hard, and she does her very best to keep us afloat, financially, but if we would have to rent our own apartment – provided one were available, she couldn't make the payments.

For Christmas, Mama sews doll dresses from her customers' scrap materials. One is for Gisela's doll, one for mine. This is all she can afford to give us. We are delighted.

Tante Käthe, Tante Dora, and Tante Lotte have gifts for us, too. One hands us a pencil, the other a tiny notepad, and the third one has bought us a ruled notebook for our schoolwork. All Christmas presents are received with great delight.

For a while, during the cold months, our school serves hot soups to all pupils. The food is a donation from the American Quaker Society, and the rotund butcher, who has prepared it, delivers it to us in big kettles. Oh, it is wonderful to be handed a bowl of thin vegetable or rice soup, and even when watered-down oatmeal gruel is dished out, we love it. But ... sometimes ... better not look ... maggots swim around in our soup. We push them aside. I shudder. I think I can't do it, but then I close my eyes and bravely eat the food anyhow. Even when we find the disgusting, white, tiny things floating around in our bowls, we are thankful that someone cares.

Somehow, the cruel winter passes. In the spring, whenever we find time, Mama, Gisela, and I undertake the hour-long walk to our piece of property on Fleischerstraße in Rudow to get the ground ready for planting. We have turnip seeds, and we are determined to have a crop this year. Perhaps, we have a few other seeds, too, but I really can't remember. All I recall are the many hikes to Rudow to tend the garden, and then the bountiful harvest of turnips, the yellow rutabaga variety, some of them as big as a baby's head. From then on, we always try for a crop of turnips to supplement our meager food supply. When our hunger pangs are great, we gnaw on raw turnip slices, and cooked turnips are served for supper at least three times a week. Of course, we share with Oma and Opa. Though our initial supply looks enormous, it dwindles down to nothing much too quickly.

Besides scavenging for wood, we also canvass the parks for weeds to cook. Lamb's-quarter leaves taste like fine spinach. Stinging nettle, difficult to pick because it irritates the fingers, has a stronger flavor, but we make a vegetable soup out of it, which gets thickened with a grated potato.

Onkel Gerhard laughs at us and says, "All you're eating is a lot of hot water with a bit of green in it."

I don't think he realizes that a stomach full of hot water feels better than an empty stomach. So we enjoy a temporary illusion of fullness, and what's so bad about that? Can we help it that we don't have more substantial meals to eat?

In the fall, we try gleaning. Not too far away, toward Buckow, are a few potato and wheat fields. As soon as the farmers are done with their harvest, people storm the fields in hopes of finding a few leftovers. We try it, but hours of digging produce only a few potatoes the size of marbles, and the wheat field has been cleaned up by other folks already. Needless to say, our disappointment is great.

*

In 1946, I begin confirmation classes. Under normal circumstances, I should've had instructions since age twelve and been confirmed by now. Since so many youngsters are behind schedule, the church accepts us latecomers for a shortened term. Instead of the usual two years of classes, we will only have one.

Once a week, a large group of boys and girls now crowds into the small room off the sanctuary, the vestry. Our religious training is worth mentioning.

The pastor takes attendance, and every week it's the same.

"Christa!"

"Here."

"Have you been in church last Sunday?"

"Yes"

"Good." He marks his book.

"Peter!"

"Here."

"Have you been in church last Sunday?"

"No."

"Why not?"

"I've been sick."

"Sick again? You seem to be sick a lot."

"Yes, *Herr Pfarrer.*"

"I'm glad you're better today."

Our religious leader frowns, shakes his head, and scribbles in his book.

And so it goes until our hour is just about over, and we only have time to listen to a morsel of instruction and a short prayer.

For several weeks, we have lessons with the sisters of the evangelical diocese, in their motherhouse, and, instead of taking attendance, they teach us a number of passages from the Bible, psalms, and hymns. We also get homework. What we have to memorize for the next week, I recite on my way home. I'm a quick learner. If a passerby hears me talking to myself and thinks I'm crazy, I don't care. I do the same babbling while walking when I have to learn poetry or vocabulary for school. It saves a lot of time.

Shortly before confirmation, our dear pastor realizes that his class has not received much teaching from him. We know just about nothing. Quickly, very quickly, he tries to jam the most basic information about the Lutheran belief into our brains.

Our important date is in the fall of 1947. A week prior to that, we have to have an exam with the parents present. Our pastor doesn't want to look like a fool, and we, his students, are supposed to impress our fathers, mothers, and the people from the church council.

"If you know the answer, raise your right hand. If you don't know the answer, raise your left hand. I will only pick on those with the right hand up. Make sure you all have a hand up, either one." He is not satisfied until we assure him that the rule is understood.

Our exam goes as planned. We all pass. But what does God have to say about deceit?

By now, Mama has given up most of her sewing at home. Frau Hintze, the boss from her days of apprenticeship to the time she has had to quit to raise a family, has just opened her shop again and rehired my mother, who is happy to be back in the old, familiar workplace. Mama is also very proud to be put in charge of the new apprentices. Working for Frau Hintze has an added advantage. Mama gets hold of a piece of black material for my confirmation dress. Yes, I'll be received into the church, as confirmed member, wearing the customary black dress. And Mama buys me a tiny bouquet of white flowers with a short, white veil attached to it – also customary, which I will carry in my hands.

My confirmation calls for a celebration to which the relatives will be invited. What can we serve them? They expect cake. Our allotted rations barely

213

keep us alive, and so we cannot even consider using our precious food stamps for ingredients to bake something for a number of guests. My mother, probably having mulled over the situation for weeks, perhaps even months, comes up with a brilliant idea.

"We will gather acorns," she declares one sunny day.

So we take some bags and head for the old section of Britz, the area where the church and our school are located. That's where the streets are lined with oak trees, and where the acorns are now littering the ground. Mama, Gisela, and I gather up an awful lot of acorns. This is the easy part. What follows is much harder. We have to crack open all those nuts, and then Mama cooks them and drains the water off, and then she cooks them a few more times until, finally, she decides that all the bitterness must be cooked out and discarded with the water. After that, the acorns are put in the warm oven to dry. And then Mama grinds them like regular nuts.

Our garden crop this year has not only yielded turnips but also red beets. When cooked, those beets give off a red juice. Sacrifice some sugar, add it to the red liquid, and, voila, something resembling cherry juice has been concocted. A thickener is needed. For that, Mama soaks our and Oma's potato peels in water. After a while, she removes the peels and waits until the water has evaporated. The white residue is potato starch, a proper thickener for the beet juice.

Our guests are greatly pleased with my mother's special creation, a torte with a thick, very nutty crust and a jiggling, red, fruity topping. When our pastor drops by later that afternoon, he also gets a piece of the wonderful cake my mother has baked. I doubt that he knows what he's eating.

"He has a feast day. He makes his rounds to all the celebrations." Oma seems to know our pastor's habits.

The next day, right after school, I have to put on my confirmation outfit again, take my flowers, and present myself to the neighbors and to the shop owners in our area. This is the custom. People expect your visit, and you should not deprive them of the opportunity to admire you and to express their congratulations and best wishes. For this privilege, they give you a bit of money. Also, from now on, they address you as an adult. When the first person I visit, a friendly, elderly shoemaker, but not the one who later loses my shoes, calls me Fräulein Eva instead of just Eva, I almost burst out laughing. I still feel like a little girl, not like a young miss. Oh, well, I will get used to my new status.

*

It is in 1947, shortly after confirmation, I believe, when, in art class, we have the assignment of illustrating *Thumbelina*, the fairy tale. We are working with watercolors. Lots of moaning and groaning is going on, especially from the boys. I'm having fun. When all my pages are finished, the

215

teacher is so impressed that he submits my work to a scholastic magazine. It gets published.

Something else is being added to our curriculum, and it is wonderful: Music. Our new teacher is a short, stocky fellow, still fairly young, quite talented, and full of enthusiasm. We call him Momo, but not to his face. I'm pretty sure that word of his nickname has come to him rather quickly, but he doesn't let on to it. Why do we call him Momo? Because all our vocal exercises are being done using the syllables mo, mo, mo. Not ever do we sing la, la, la or mi, mi, mi or anything else.

One day, while in the process of erasing notes from the blackboard, Momo suddenly turns around to face the class and announces, "When I see you again, we're having auditions. Prepare a song."

We are perplexed. We would like to ask questions. Our teacher gives us no chance. He leaves the room.

The following week, when it is time for our music class, we sit in our seats, speculating, and waiting for the things to come.

Momo enters. Without wasting a minute, he gets down to business. He begins with the first person in the front and goes down the row. Everyone has to sing a brief solo. He places this girl in one corner, that one in another, and the boys all the way to the back of the room. It makes sense; sopranos, altos, male voices. Christa, my best friend beams as she is told where to go.

216

Now it is my turn. I sing the first verse of an old folksong.

"Remain in your seat," Momo tells me.

Am I this bad? I think. I feel terrible, humiliated.

When Rosemarie from the next row is also told to sit back down, I'm really perplexed. She has a beautiful voice, in my opinion. I glance at her, she glances back, and we both shake our sorrowful heads.

Eventually, the solo renditions are over. Now our teacher makes each group sing alone. He switches certain students from one corner to another. Then the sections sing together. Apparently satisfied with his evaluation, Momo orders all pupils back to their seats. Christa is still beaming; I try to avoid eye contact with her.

We sit in silence, waiting for our teacher to explain what this has been about.

He clears his throat. Then he speaks. "I'm forming a small concert choir. Rosemarie and Eva are in it."

I wonder if I've heard correctly. Quickly, I look to Rosemarie. She nods and smiles.

About a week later, we have the first rehearsal. Our choir consists of about twenty-five singers of various ages. Some are weeded out a bit later, Rosemarie among them. I feel bad for her. What we sing is beautiful, especially the choruses from *Cavalleria Rusticana* and *Pagliacci*. I adore opera music.

My dear friend must be very disappointed, but she doesn't say a word. We avoid the subject on the way home from school. I don't think she ever shows envy.

In sixth grade high school, we are required to take physics and chemistry. Since we have no lab facility in our little school building, we walk to the big elementary school and then do experiments over there. Labs bore me. The teacher only calls on the boys to mix chemicals and to use vials, petri dishes and Bunsen burners. My male classmates crowd around the work counter, and they are able to witness the chemical reactions. The girls are banned to their seats and see nothing but the boys' backs. Then we take notes of what is reported by the ones doing the work up front. Honestly, it isn't fair. Maybe, the teacher doesn't believe girls are interested in science. I'm glad that calculating formulas can be done on paper, a job deemed suitable for girls, yet despised by many. But, actually, it's just a form of math with a chemical twist, and I love math.

Physics, to me, is a dry subject. I memorize the facts. Some laws make sense; others clutter my mind for a while and then disappear until restudied for an exam.

*

Life with my little cousin hasn't gotten any easier. Gisela and I still watch her when Tante Gertrud is at work. Now that Christa is older and knows how to talk, she has turned into a great liar. Since we are not allowed to spank her, we try to put some fear into her.

"Look at the floor over there," I say, pointing at the few feet of hallway that separate the kitchen from our bedroom. "When you don't tell the truth, the floor will open up, and you will fall through. Is that what you want, Christa?"

"No," she bawls, and then she refuses to cross from one room to the other.

One afternoon, when I have to take her along to run an errand, she wrenches her little hand from mine and darts away from me, in the middle of the street. Usually, the street is pretty much free of traffic, but this time, a car is approaching, and I fear for my cousin's safety. I lunge forward, pull her out of harm's way, but fall down myself. In the process, I knock out a front tooth. It is still dangling by the root, and I hold it with my fingers, for I don't want to lose it. After putting Christa in Oma's and Gisela's care, I'm off to the dentist. Fortunately, he is able to reattach my tooth, but the nerve is dead and, as a constant reminder of my cousin's naughtiness, I have to live with a lifeless front tooth.

Dental care in the years following the war is a nightmare. Woe the one with a toothache! In the absence of Novocain, the dentist drills until he hits a nerve and the patient cannot tolerate the pain any more. Then he stops and plugs the hole with cotton soaked in an analgesic agent. A week later, he drills some more. This continues until all decay is removed.   In case of a deep cavity, the drilling process may go on for more than a month. Then comes the filling, a temporary one first, later the permanent one.

Of course, little Christa is not always a holy terror. She's probably no worse than other children her age. Sometimes, I even enjoy her company, and I like to do nice things for her. When it's her naptime, she wants me to tell her stories. That's my fault, because I have gotten her into the habit. Gisela, not wanting to miss this daily story time, lies down, too. Usually we're all on the bed together with our little cousin. Every day, I spin a new story about elves and witches, and little boys and girls, and about animal characters and whatever else pops into my head.

When Christa is eager to know more about the elves, I tell her we have some living in our cellar.

"I want to see them," she declares.

"Okay," I say, "I'll take you with me the next time I have to go down there to get something."

When she's not looking, I draw tiny elves resembling Santa's helpers, cut them out, go into the basement and place the paper figures on top of some old bags and boxes.

Every tenant has a small, locked place in the basement. To get to my grandparents' cubicle, I have to walk down a long, dark hallway, and this is spooky. When alone, I'm a bit afraid that some evil character might lurk around the bend. Then I pretend I have other people following me.

"Come on, Gerhard, let's go," I say in a rather loud voice. "Peter will be here in a minute." I use any name that pops into my head and hope the presence of two invented males will deter a would-be attacker. In the many years my grandparents have occupied their apartment, not a single person has been harmed in the house, neither in the dark basement nor upstairs, to the best of my knowledge. Still, I want to play it safe.

Needless to say, the display of the elves is a great success. Christa is delighted. By this time, Onkel Gerhard has changed jobs. He doesn't work for the bread company anymore, but now test-drives automobiles. So, one fine day, he takes Mama, Gisela, and me along for a ride. We are going all the way to Opa's place of birth, which is Halle on the Saale, in Saxony, where we will visit relatives.

Our joy is great. We laugh and sing most of the way, except when we have to stop, which happens frequently, and Onkel Gerhard has to add more water to the battery. Honestly, this car is not ready to be offered for sale, for it constantly overheats. It definitely needs fixing first.

When we get to Halle, the aunt and uncle, both unknown to Gisela and me, welcome us kindly. They must've been notified of our coming, because a cake is waiting for us. Chocolate cake! It is a delicious treat, something we haven't had in years. And Gisela, the shy one, surprises us all by asking for a second piece. She gets it.

Then we all take a walk through the city. When we come to the marvelous, wide steps leading up to the bridge that crosses the Saale River, Mama shows us where, as a child, she has "accidentally" lost the often-talked-about piece of onion cake, a treat bought for her by the aunt. Onion cake, in certain parts of Germany, is an autumn specialty.

"It fell out of my hand, I told my aunt," says my mother, "and she believed it. There was no way I could get myself to eat it. Onion cake … ugh!"

*

It is late in the year, I believe, or, perhaps, already a few months into 1948, when I finally realize that, indeed, I'm not a little girl anymore. The braids will have to go. All the other girls in my class have done away with theirs long ago, and they sport modern hairdos. When I mention it to Mama, she agrees that I should have my hair cut and get a perm to look more fashionable. I hate to take the money from her for something so frivolous.

When the hair from my long braids falls to the floor, I look at my lost tresses with some regret. The hairdresser teasingly asks me, if she should glue them back on, and then she rolls what is left of my crowning glory on skinny curling rods, applies a stinky solution, and attaches a multitude of electrical wires to the rods. It looks ridiculous, like giant spider legs clinging to my head. I don't remember all the steps required for this curly hairstyle, but when it's

222

all finished, I'm well pleased with the new me. People tell me, I look very pretty.

I guess this is really the time of my growing up. With it comes the chance for my first paycheck.

Next door live the Beckers. They have a son who's in elementary school, third or fourth grade. This boy, Heinz, is involved in a traffic accident, and he is unable to go to classes for several weeks. The insurance company is willing to pay for a tutor for as long as he can't walk to school. Would I want to teach the boy? Of course! Heinz is a diligent student, and with my help, he keeps up with all his class work. In the end, I submit my bill, and the check comes in the mail. Now I can pay for some of my own expenses, which makes it easier on Mama, and I feel so good about it.

But my mother has secretly stashed away a small fund, too, for a very special purpose. One day, she springs the big surprise on me.

"Evchen," she says, "you will be taking lessons in ballroom dancing. I will register you at Meisel's School of Dance in Neukölln."

"Dance lessons?" I ask. I think I haven't heard correctly.

"Yes," says my mother. "Every girl should learn to dance."

"It costs too much money," I protest.

"Not that much. Meisel's isn't as expensive as some other schools."

Since I've heard from several girls in my class that they, too, will begin dance lessons, but at Geisler's, the more expensive studio, I'm willing to embark on the new adventure.

In the meantime, the situation in Berlin has changed a bit for the better, and people seem to be confident that the future will be even brighter. I guess that my mother, too, is filled with optimism.

Frau Meisel, the owner of the dance school, is an elderly lady. Her dancing days are over, and she is now in charge of the paperwork. Her daughter, Inge Meisel-Karras, and son-in-law, a striking, talented couple, have taken over the teaching. Those two, plus a few very advanced students, regularly participate in national competitions. Pupils with lesser experience, especially the beginners, view them with awe.

Classes, as a rule, are held in the ballroom, where the wooden dance floor is always polished to a high gloss. Chairs are set up on opposite sides of the room, along the walls, so that the male students have to face the young ladies.

The girls are eager to get started, but the fellows need some prodding. Once they are made to understand that they are expected to participate, to choose partners, politely bow and ask for the dance, they stop being glued to their chairs. After each number, the girls have to be escorted back to their chairs and properly thanked.

We get instructions on how to do the waltz – slow and Viennese, the polka, the foxtrot, and the tango. Oh, yes, we also do the two-step, which the Germans call the march, the easiest dance of all. I don't think anybody needs instructions for this one, because you simply have to step to the music … one two, one two … all around the dance floor.

A musician, using an old, black piano on the stage, bangs out the tunes. His repertoire is not very extensive. He probably doesn't get paid very much.

I enjoy every lesson, and when my mother signs me up for the second session, I am delighted.

From time to time, special classes are being offered for the Latin dances, and I'm allowed to attend those, too. My favorite is the rumba.

I continue going to Meisel's for several years, but not as a student. After having finished the second set of weeks, I volunteer to be a helper. The teacher can always use a few experienced ladies to gently – or rather forcefully - guide her least talented male students around the dance floor. Some of the young men need an awful lot of prodding and pushing and counting out the steps. Keeping up the rhythm while sorting out their left foot from their right seems to be too difficult for individuals not blessed with a natural talent for dancing. Fortunately, the helpers also have an occasional chance to be paired with young men who have excellent timing and don't get their feet all tangled up. We live for those moments.

When we have a Sunday afternoon or evening social, I never sit out a dance. I guess I'm as popular as my mother has been in her younger days.

"All the men wanted to dance with me," she tells Gisela and me. "Because of my sparkling eyes, my girlfriends told me. But I was also light on my feet, and that helped."

Since I have sparkling eyes and light feet, too, the young men probably don't notice my not very glamorous, not even fashionable clothes. Sometimes, my mother lets me wear her white dress with the flower print, which looks pretty on me. But, please, don't look at my shoes! I only own one pair, and they have holes.

When Mama comes up with a piece of leather from some unknown source, she takes my shoes to the shoemaker to have new soles put on.

"Are the shoes ready?" she asks a few days later.

The man looks at her, and then he looks at me, and then he shakes his head in a sorrowful way. "I'm so sorry, Frau Beetz," he says. "Somebody broke into my shop and stole your daughter's shoes. There's nothing I can do about it. I'm really sorry."

"I don't believe it!" shouts my mother.

"I'm telling the truth," he insists, wringing his hands.

"He sold them, I'm sure," says my mother as soon as we are out of his shop.

From then on, I have to wear Mama's shoes, the ones she has lent me already for the few days my own shoes have been away for repairs. Now she is left with just the ones she has on her feet.

*

The summer of 1948 brings big changes. In order to get Germany's industry back on its feet, a monetary reform is being implemented. On June 20, all current money, the *Reichsmark*, has to be turned in. Forty new German marks, *DM*, short for *Deutsche Mark*, per person are given out.

Four days later, on June 24, the Soviets close all roads leading into the West sectors of Berlin. No goods can reach us by land or river. Wanting to rule the whole city, the Russians hope to starve us into submission. But the Western powers are not ready to hand us over, and so, just two days into the blockade, the Americans orchestrate a humanitarian airlift to keep us alive. They send their planes, affectionately called *Rosinenbomber*, raisin bombers, with food supplies. Those bombers land in Tempelhof, only a few miles from where we live, and their constant roar in the sky becomes a welcome sound.

The store shelves and bins are emptier than ever. When a delivery is made ... or expected, word gets around, and customers rush to stand in long lines. Sometimes, everything is sold out before the last weary person gets to the door. My mother, after walking home from work, is often too worn and weak from hunger to stand in line for our meager food rations.

Oma, Gisela and I go to the parks again, almost daily, to pick weeds for cooking. Once, we almost poison the whole family by using the tiny leaves of a low growing plant, *Scharbockskraut,* ranunculus, also known as creeping buttercup, which we have found quite tasty before. To our surprise, our cooked greenery has a bitter flavor. A short time after finishing our meal, we experience stomach pains and vomiting. Later, we learn that the plant is only edible, in small amounts, before it begins to bloom in the spring. Of course, we have seen the tiny blossoms. How can something so pretty cause poisoning?

More than ever, we are looking forward to our annual turnip crop. Once or twice, on our walk home from Rudow, we snitch a few carrots from a farmer's field. We feel terrible for stealing, but the vegetables taste mighty good. On one occasion, we also harvest some forbidden ears of corn. Actually, we have no idea what to do with them, for this kind of vegetable has never been sold in our stores. Mama removes the husks and then boils the corn … and keeps on boiling it, but it doesn't get tender. Finally, we eat it the way it is. It takes a lot of chewing. No, we will never steal corn again. When we talk about it later, we are informed that we have been eating horse corn. Horses have bigger teeth than humans, and their stomachs are made to digest such hard fare.

Off and on, I have private students who need tutoring in English, French, or math. Somehow, word gets around in school that I'm the one who can help the lower-grade kids who are falling behind in their work due to missed lessons or slowness in learning. I like teaching, and one of my instructors insists I should make it my profession. She may be right. I have to give it some thought. Later.

Summer vacation comes around, and I hear about a new program for younger children. They can go to day camp. A bus will pick them up every morning, just two blocks down the street from me, and take them to the athletic field in Rudow. Camp counselors are needed, and I'm old enough to apply. What an opportunity to spend a few weeks outdoors and earn money besides! I apply. I get the job.

Now, each weekday morning, at the bus stop, I do roll call of my young charges, and then we head for our campground. We have picked a big, shady tree to be our gathering place, and that's where we sing, tell stories, and have all those activities, which require no roaming. At times, various groups come together for ballgames. When athletic competitions or scavenger hunts are scheduled, all campers participate.

As farewell activity, a big show is on the agenda. Each group has to perform something.

What can my kids do? I think hard. *Aha! Summer of 1943. Bansin.*

I remember the musical piece of the kidnapped fairy and the elves. As soon as I give a little description of it to my girls, they are excited and eager to get started. Since we don't have enough people to fill the roles, I ask permission to have the neighboring group join us. I think the other counselor is relieved that she doesn't have to figure out something for her own gaggle of girls. Our offering turns out to be a success. The kids are happy; I'm proud of them.

Parting time is hard. Tears are rolling down many cheeks. I get more hugs than I've had in an eternity.

*

Nineteen forty-eight is the year when I become a tenth grader. This doesn't happen until summer vacation is over. Up to 1944, the school year has always begun in spring, but since the chaos of 1945 has caused an interruption in education all over Germany, school calendars have been changed.

Momo's new lesson plan calls for teaching us music technique. He explains composition and four-part harmony. I only comprehend half of it. In my opinion, I'm a dunce. I copy every example Momo puts on the board. When we are assigned to add the harmony notes to a basic musical phrase, I match them to the examples. I get away with it, but I have no idea how the process really works.

We also have to hand in an original composition – a small one. Somehow, mine turns out well enough. But I'm terribly happy when we get back to just singing. I'm not a musical genius, just a girl who loves to exercise her vocal cords.

In German literature class, we are into poetry. We have to learn many famous pieces by heart. One day, it is my turn to recite *Der Knabe im Moor (The Boy in the Fen)* by Annette von Droste-Hülshoff. This is a rather eerie poem, spine tingling, when done with proper feeling. I give it my all. Soon I notice how Herr Bierbaum, the teacher, drops his head onto his folded hands on the desk, and he stares at me in the weirdest way.

Why is he leaning forward like this? His eyes are ready to roll out of his head! Is he okay? I think. My teacher scares me a bit, but I do not dare to stop my recitation.

I finish the poem. There's a long silence.

Finally, Herr Bierbaum sits up straight. He leans back in his chair. He slowly comes out of his trance. "Marvelous," he says.

Now it dawns on me. *I had him mesmerized!*

From then on, at special school gatherings, I have to recite poetry for large audiences. I have butterflies in my stomach each time, but as soon as I get started, my mind is on the words and the mood. It feels, as if I'm transported into another realm.

I really like Herr Bierbaum. He is a good, caring teacher. When the winter weather sets in, and our school turns very, very cold, he takes us on a wood-scavenging hike. He even lets us cut down small trees – with or without permission. Thanks to his initiative, we get heat into our classroom, and that feels so wonderful.

It begins to snow. We are reminded of the very important rule that the throwing of snowballs is strictly forbidden in the schoolyard. But the white, beautiful snow beckons. One of the boys from the upper class cannot resist. He forms a ball; he throws it; it hits Fräulein Wittenberg's head. The old spinster – I assume she is a spinster – is outraged. She demands punishment of the culprit. The poor fellow, so close to graduation, is expelled from our school.

*

One evening, Gisela declares, "We have to bake cookies. Christmas will be here soon."

"I'm sorry, but we can't," replies my mother. "If we use the ration stamps for flour, we won't have bread to eat."

Gisela looks crushed. She is still so childlike at age fourteen, whereas I already consider myself a tough realist, hardened by the miseries of previous years.

The next days pass as usual. My sister and I trudge to school and shiver as the icy winds blow around street corners and through the ruins. We huddle in our cold classrooms, pulling our shabby coats tighter. At home, we complete our daily chores and then, when the electricity fails, settle by the light of the foul-smelling carbide lamp to do our assignments. We call this lamp our *Knallerballer*, because it has the habit of giving off explosive noises. On occasion, a bigger than usual bang occurs, and this frightens us a little.

*

As Christmas is almost upon us, and we are all gathered around the kitchen table, Gisela brings over her schoolbag and pulls out a mysterious bundle. Smiling triumphantly, she opens it, turns it over, and lets several pieces of stale bread fall out.

I gape in disbelief.

Mama shakes her head and says, "But that's the bread you were supposed to eat in school. That's your lunches. Are you sick?" She looks really worried.

"I want you to get flour ... for Christmas cookies," Gisela stammers. "If we all share this bread ... for a few days ... you won't have to buy a new loaf. You can use the stamps for flour instead."

So it happens, thanks to my sister's sacrifice, that Mama is able to mix cookie dough. And when the delicious fragrance of baked goods permeates the apartment, we are excited and full of the holiday spirit.

I have begged to use a small piece of dough to shape into a special creation for Gisela. When it is baked and presented to her, she looks at it in wonderment and asks, "What is it?"

"Don't you see? It's a pair of eyeglasses."

"What for?"

"So you can see better. You always tell us your helpings of food are larger than ours, and than you want to give us some of yours to make them even. Perhaps, with those glasses on, you will be able to recognize what is in front of you."

Honestly, my sister is too gentle and unselfish for her own good.

The following morning, we wake up to a surprise. Snow has fallen. It blankets the city streets. It covers the jagged ruins and the ugly rubble heaps. Parks are transformed into winter wonderlands. Nature is oblivious to political boundaries and, in total disregard of the blockade, has blessed us, the isolated inhabitants of the western occupation sectors, with the same beauty as our fellow citizens that belong to the East.

After school, Gisela and I join our friends in a merry snowball fight. We frolic in the white fluff until our hands turn red and stiff, and our feet feel as if they might fall off from frostbite.

Then arrives the last day of classes before the holidays. Our teacher lights four candles on a Christmas wreath. We sing carols. A few of us recite poetry. Before we depart, we wish each other a merry Christmas.

*

December 24 begins quite ordinary. First comes the usual housecleaning, which Gisela and I try to complete in record time. After that, we roam the streets for firewood. When we can't find enough there, we go to the ruins and unearth some sticks and pieces of tarpaper from under the snow and the rough stones.

By the time we come back to the apartment, Mama has returned from work, and she asks, "Would you want to come along to pick up a bit of holiday greenery?"

"Sure," we say and drop our scavenger finds into the wood box by the stove.

We go to the coal yard, where a few Christmas trees rest against the fence. Prices are high, and we can't even afford the smallest tree. So we gather loose branches, for which the salesman charges us a few pennies. Gleefully, we carry our purchase home.

"Ingenuity is what you need," says Mama as she pokes holes into an old broomstick. Then she jams the spruce branches into these holes, and soon we have our little Christmas tree. After long metal rods with candleholders at the end are screwed into the broomstick trunk, my mother affixes white candle stubs left over from previous years. Finally, Gisela and I trim the branches with some of Oma's ornaments and tinsel. When done, we stand back in admiration. Yes, we have, indeed, the most beautiful Christmas tree.

We attend Christmas Eve service at the *Britzer Dorfkirche*. During the sermon, Gisela begins to cry. "I miss Papa so much," she sobs. I hold her hand. Mama leans over and puts her arm around her. I hear her whisper into Gisela's ear, "I miss him too."

As we step out of the church, fresh snow greets us. It dances in the air and then floats to the ground ever so gently. It settles on our hats and hair and noses, and we stick out our tongues to catch the tiny, descending flakes. We scoop up handfuls of snow and playfully toss them at each other. Gisela's tears are forgotten, and we laugh all the way home.

After soup for supper, we are ready to celebrate around our Christmas tree. Of course, Oma and Opa have to come into our room. While the candles are burning, we sing carols, and even Opa, who is usually very quiet, joins in. Then we gather around the table and feast on cookie hearts and jingle bells, and we drink *Muckefuck*, an imitation coffee made from roasted barley or some other grain.

We are truly blessed. We have cookies made with love, thanks to Gisela's sacrifice. We have a broomstick tree, Mama's wonderful creation. But best of all, we have each other. And we have God, who watches over us, and who will never allow anybody to take Christmas away from us, not even the Russians.

*

Early in the year of 1949, I come down with a terrible cold. My chest hurts; I have a high fever; I'm very weak. My mother walks to the doctor and asks for help. Since he refuses to make a house call, she has to drag me to his office. We have to wait for hours to be seen.

"Eva has pneumonia," he determines at last. "Take her home and put her to bed."

Soon, I feel as if I'm burning up. I become delirious. No prescription medicine is available. Mama hovers over me, constantly giving me sips of water, putting wet cloths on my forehead, and wrapping my legs with cool, damp towels. In my subconscious state, I know she's there, but I'm too out of it to acknowledge her presence. How long I'm in critical condition, I do not know. But when I finally come to recognize my surroundings again, I see the tired, yet beaming face of my mother, and it makes me happy.

"I got you over the crisis," she sighs. "Now you will get better."

Oh, I'm still so very weak. I can't even get out of bed. But, suddenly, I remember something, and it seems extremely important.

"When is the masked ball?" I ask.

"Tomorrow."

"Tomorrow? I have to be out of bed by then. I have to go to the ball."

Why does Mama give me such a funny smile? Doesn't she know I'm serious? I've been looking forward to the masked ball for a long time. It's going to be my very first one. I can't miss it. I want to dance the night away."

I try to sit up. I can't. I'm so very, very tired. For now, I have to forget about the masked ball. Sleep is more important.

Of course, I cannot dance the next day. I cannot even stand up properly. It takes a while until I get some of my strength back. When I finally venture out of the house, I have to lean on my mother. My weight is a mere 66 lbs, and I'm almost seventeen years old. With our meager food rations, it takes a long time until I put on a few pounds again.

And then another discomfort hits me. Each step I take hurts. My shoes, the ones inherited from my mother, pinch badly. No matter how much I curl my toes, the torture doesn't go away.

When I finally dare to tell Mama the bad news, she's at a loss.

Oma soon finds out about my problem. She leaves the room. A few minutes later, she reappears, a pair of her shoes in hand.

"Here, try them on," she says and hands me the sturdy, extra wide, black shoes, the kind old ladies wear for comfort.

"They are rather big," I say, "but I can pull the laces tight, and then they won't fall off. But, Oma, are you sure you can spare them?

"Yes, yes, take them. See, I still have shoes on my feet."

I thank my grandmother profusely. I don't care if my feet are not stylishly shod. Nobody in school ridicules me for my footwear, and when I go back to dancing, I'm as popular as before I switched to those big, extra-wide, clunky, black shoes.

*

I'm barely back on my feet again, when the big move from our small schoolhouse in Old Britz to the much bigger *Onkel-Bräsig-Schule* in the newer section of Britz comes about. This school, used as a field hospital during the war, has finally been renovated and released to the school system. Some of my male classmates assist with the transport of books and lab equipment. A few parents volunteer, too.

Now, I can stroll to my lessons under shady Japanese cherry trees, or I may walk through the park that abuts the school grounds. The path winds alongside a lake, and the sight of water, lawns, trees, and many, many rambling roses is beautiful.

Our new facilities are spacious. For almost every class we switch rooms. We have a chemistry lab, where, again, the teacher or the boys do the experiments, and the girls have to watch. In the biology room, thank goodness, even the girls are allowed to touch Hugo, the rattling skeleton, to identify his bones. On big charts, we locate muscles, arteries, and organs.

We have an art room and a music room. For reasons unknown, wonderful Momo has not made the move with us. Our new teacher disbands the concert choir and starts up a chorus, which all interested students may join. No audition is needed.

In the huge gym, we use the equipment. I'm glad the teacher doesn't ask us to perform splits and other gymnastic tricks on the mat. I'm definitely not floor exercise material.

*

And then, all of a sudden, on May 12, 1949, the Soviets lift the blockade. The roads are open again, railroad and waterway traffic resumes, and we breathe freedom. Goods pour into the western-occupied sectors of the city. The shelves are being stocked with food, wonderful, glorious food! The electricity stays on. Heating material is available. Stores have clothes for sale. As long as money is available, people can buy almost anything.

Oh, what a wonderful feeling! Life promises to be good again.

CHAPTER FIVE

THE NEW DAWN

Toward the end of the school year, we go on a class trip, the very first one ever. We take a train to the outskirts of Berlin, and we make ourselves at home under shady trees near a restaurant and a boat rental place. The lake in front of us beckons. With our teacher's permission, some of my classmates rent rowboats, and they seem to have great fun on the water.

"Should we try it, too?" asks Christa, my girlfriend.

"Did you ever handle a boat before?" I want to know. "I have no idea how."

"Neither have I," she confesses. "But it can't be very hard."

"Okay then, let's go."

Soon we drag our rented boat to the edge of the water. We climb into the wobbly craft and get it afloat without tipping. Rowing straight out into the lake is no problem. By trial and error, we eventually turn the boat to the right, parallel to the coastline. Should we run into trouble, we might stand a better chance to get rescued when not far away from land.

"How much time do you think we have left?"

"Oh, about fifteen more minutes," Christa guesses.

Neither one of us owns a watch.

"Maybe we should turn back," I suggest.

"Okay."

"How?"

"I don't know." Christa shrugs.

So we put our oars in the water, this way, that way, and nothing good comes of it. Christa handles the front; I'm in the back. Precious time slips by, and we're not getting anywhere. We are pretty much at wit's end when, suddenly, quite by accident, we discover the correct maneuver. The boat turns.

Now we row like crazy. We get the boat back to the rental place with barely a minute to spare.

"How was it?" some of our friends ask.

"It was beautiful," we declare. Of course, we keep it a secret that we still don't know how to steer a boat. Nobody has to know.

*

School lets out for the summer. Some of my classmates and I are invited to a garden party, given by Christel, who lives in Buckow, in a very nice house, untouched by the war. Her father is a baker, and he has so generously provided the food for our celebration. Music comes from a record player. We dance. The evening air is balmy; the outdoor lights are dim; the mood is carefree.

As I'm standing on the sideline, having a friendly conversation with one of the fellows, he pulls me close and plants a kiss on my lips. It takes me by surprise. This is my very first kiss, and I have no idea how to respond. I don't even know if I like it. The

242

longer I think about it, the more I'm convinced I can do without kissing. Besides, Mama has always preached to never get involved with someone from school or from work. It only leads to trouble.

I cannot recall much of that summer other than that Gisela and her girlfriend, Marianne, are always off to the dirty canal for swimming, and I frequent the newly opened American library in Rudow. Having access to big, fat books, written in the English language, is marvelous.

In August, toward the end of school vacation, Mama sends me to Mittweida in Saxony to visit Tante Uschi. My aunt is a wonderful hostess and an excellent cook. She tries to spoil me. Though big with child, her first one, she shows me around the area almost daily. We walk a lot, mainly through the woods and up and down the gentle hillside. Once, she slips and falls, and I'm greatly afraid the tumble might cause her to deliver on the spot. Nothing bad happens, thank God.

I also get to see Großer Opa, his new, young wife, and his latest set of children. The two little boys are in a playpen.

"Meet your Tante Evchen," says my grandfather to Bernd, about two years of age, and roughly one-year-old Herbert.

I laugh. Tante Uschi gets the giggles.

"I'm not their aunt," I correct my grandfather. "They are my uncles!"

Martha, his wife, agrees. Großer Opa looks perplexed. After all, it doesn't happen every day that the uncles are younger than their niece.

Later that day, my grandfather proudly shows me his new factory in town. He, the former maker of fancy combs, is now manufacturing buttons of many shapes and sizes from animal horns. I believe he also produces combs again, but I'm not sure.

While I'm in Mittweida, Onkel Martin pops in over the weekend. He has come to check on his wife and to report, I assume, how the setting up of their apartment in Berlin is coming along. Friends in the Steglitz district, real close to the Botanical Gardens, have given my uncle a job in their bakery and a place to stay above the store. It will be nice to have Tante Uschi in Berlin again. And soon I will have a brand-new cousin there, too.

"I have a surprise waiting at home," says my mother when she picks me up from the train station a few days later.

"What is it?"

"Just wait and see."

Oh, am I curious!

We get home, and after I have greeted everybody, Mama shows me a tiny, strange-looking gadget sitting on the windowsill. It's mainly a flat box with crystals and wires, and I have not the slightest idea what it might be.

"Put the end pieces in your ears," says my mother.

I do. I hear music. I'm amazed. This is wonderful!

*

It's the beginning of my senior year in high school. Our desks are set up in horseshoe fashion, and I'm sitting near the door, facing the windows. Our class has shrunk to less than twenty students. Some have not been promoted; others have quit on their own. Among the latter, as it turns out, is my best friend. For the first few days, I 'm puzzled by her absence. As far as I know, she's not sick. Why is she not in school? Finally, I stop by her apartment to find out what's going on.

"They notified my parents that I wouldn't pass, and so my mother transferred me to another school," she confesses, sheepishly.

"Where to?"

"Neukölln."

"And they put you with the seniors?"

"Yes."

Oh, well, I think, *Neukölln has a reputation for not being very particular. Anybody who can't make it in Britz has a chance there.*

"Why didn't you tell me?"

She shrugs. No explanation. I know the answer. She has been too embarrassed to admit her failure. But I wonder how long she would've tried to avoid me.

The matter is in the open, and nothing stands in the way of our friendship. With lenient teachers and a soft marking system, she will finish her senior year and graduate. I work as hard as ever to follow the strict curriculum of my school, the one known for its excellence.

In mathematics, we are into advanced algebra. Herr Kästner, our teacher, stands at the blackboard, scribbling problems with three unknowns, x, y, and z. Most of his students can't solve them. Off and on, he gets stuck himself. Then Horst and I, the acclaimed class math wizards, join him, and the three of us put our heads together. Rows and rows of equations appear on the board. The rest of the class has no idea what we are doing. That's too bad, but we can't spend an eternity explaining. Let them copy the steps and the answers and figure the whole procedure out later.

We also work with logarithms, for which we have a book. Of course, the use of logarithm tables is only recommended for difficult calculations. Someone in class doesn't realize this, and the poor fellow looks into the book to determine how much two to the second power is. Herr Kästner cannot understand such lack of common sense.

In geometry, dipping into the field of astronomy, we figure out the paths of earth and moon and other celestial bodies and pinpoint their locations at given times. Though I have no difficulty with this part of math, I'm glad when we are back into the fun of algebra, trigonometry, and calculus.

We have a very nice, extremely intelligent deep-thinker in class, whose name is Helmut. In German literature, when the teacher asks for an interpretation of a piece of writing, Helmut speaks like a true politician. His gift of gab is amazing. By the time he is done with his answer, we, his classmates, are completely confused. Does the teacher actually understand what the young man is trying to express? Or does he only pretend to understand? Whatever the case, Helmut ends up with a good grade.

Our art teacher really gives me a hard time. He insists I should become a painter.

A painter? I think. *A starving artist? No way!*

Though I fulfill all requirements for the class, he asks for more.

"I want you to paint something every day," he says.

"I'm sorry," I answer. "I have no time. I have obligations at home."

He is furious. From now on, instead of good notes, he gives me nothing but mediocre marks. I am very upset.

When a teacher treats other students unfairly, the parents usually come to school and complain. The appearance of a father works especially well. Gisela and I have no father, and we never bother our mother with annoying school affairs, for we don't want to add to her burdens. She has enough worries already. Since Mama never shows up in school to fight for us, we are, at times, treated with little consideration. Gisela, especially, has a hard time with some teachers. I speak up, when absolutely necessary, but she is so very, very timid.

All of a sudden, something absolutely wonderful happens. Theaters and opera houses offer minimal-cost tickets to students. Filling their halls with high school kids is better than letting a number of seats go unsold. This makes sense to me. I love opera music, and I'm now allowed to attend many performances. On occasion, my classmates and I have premium seats, other times we sit in the third balcony. From so high up, we can look over the stage set and get a glimpse of what goes on behind the scenes, which is an adventure in itself. No matter where we are placed, the music is always glorious. And when we have to critique a performance as a class assignment, I gladly write my reports.

I'm picking up more students for tutoring. Children come to the apartment after school, but I also have a grown-up student who wants instructions in French, and I walk or take the trolley to her house in Rudow for the lessons. For reasons unknown, she's taking up the language at an evening school, and she needs extra help. Since she's not the brightest student, I doubt she will ever learn enough to write or converse in French. I constantly have to encourage her. When she does something right, I heap tons of praises on her. Then she jubilates like a kid.

*

Another Christmas approaches. Though we still have to pinch pennies, we are now looking forward to a holiday celebration with real cookies and a decent meal. But first, we attend a stage performance, given by Gisela's class, in the school auditorium. It's a modernized version of *Sleeping Beauty.* Gisela's tall friend plays the role of the sleeping miss. Her prince is a rather short boy. They make a comical couple. Street sweepers and women from the bucket brigade substitute courtiers and handmaidens. When poorly dressed "Sleeping Beauty" is awakened with a kiss from the little fellow, she declares, "Prince Ami, I've waited long," I get the giggles. The parents, of course, love the play, and they applaud wildly.

Gisela recites a long Christmas poem. She does a good job, honestly, but I gently criticize the way she has handled the opening line.

"It should be full of wonder," I say.

Gisela doesn't know what I'm talking about; I feel sorry I've opened my big mouth.

*

We seniors are a tight group now. We have bonded; we stick together. Could it be that we realize our days together are numbered? Graduation will soon be upon us. After that, life will take us in different directions. But first we have to deal with the dreaded final exams.

Toward the end of the school year, our teachers begin the review of everything we've learned within the last few years. Suddenly, we're supposed to recall every important date in history; be ready to name the atomic numbers of the elements, chemical formulas and reactions; remember the multitude of physical laws; know enough about the human body, animal and plant life to perhaps become a doctor, horticulturist or marine biologist; and be proficient in all phases of higher mathematics. The written exams in German literature, English and French will only consist of long essays, and that should be a fairly easy task. Everything else requires a lot of cramming, often late into the night.

To nourish my brain, Mama concocts a drink of raw egg, sugar, and red wine for me. I love it.

Before we are admitted to the final exams, we have to submit an autobiography and state our plans for the future. Teachers and certain board members evaluate our hand-ins and grades and decide who's worthy and who isn't. Ouch! A few classmates are out of the running. Now we're down to sixteen.

Our male students are worried about their Latin exam. Instead of an essay, which the girls have to do in French, they are facing the translation of a text from Latin into German. Not fond of Latin, they have not put much effort into learning the language. Oh, how they complain, how it gets them down.

Also, some of the fellows have doubts about getting through the math test.

"What can we do?" they ask one another.

"The one who finishes first asks permission to use the bathroom. He can leave a piece of paper with the answers in the stall."

"Okay."

On the day of the math test, I'm done very quickly. For safety, and because I have so much time to kill, I check my answers over and over again. I'm not allowed to leave the classroom, but I can look around.

One hand goes up. The proctor collects the student's papers for temporary safekeeping. The test taker leaves the room, and he returns, a short while later, shaking his head. Others ask to be excused. Nobody comes back with a happy smile. I assume the hatched plan of passing on information has not worked out. It is possible a teacher is in charge of checking the washroom and each stall for suspicious material before letting the next student use the facility. Even without cheating, everybody passes. Why not? Only the elite have been allowed to take the exam.

Orals follow at a later date, after the written test papers have been graded. Anybody with marks not as high as expected has to suffer the grilling by panel members, which include teachers and other qualified authorities. If, however, all written work has turned out well, the student is still subjected to one mandatory oral testing.

I am notified that I have to report for just one exam, and it will be in the subject of the panel's choice. When I find out I'll be called in for German literature, I'm relieved it isn't for chemistry or physics. Even history would be unnerving.

"Fräulein Eva Beetz …next!"

Rather jittery, I enter the room and take my seat.

The person, unknown to me, the one sitting in the center, looks at me for a while … it seems like an eternity … and then he says, "Tell us about the play you've seen a few weeks ago, *The Death of a Salesman.*"

"I'm sorry, sir," I stammer. "I didn't go to see that play. I went to the opera performance instead. Both kinds of tickets were offered to us. We had a choice. I opted for the opera."

The man shakes his head. He clears his throat. "Then … in that case … tell us about the opera."

Relieved, I give a synopsis of the musical masterpiece and explain what I have liked best and what I think has been lacking. Deep down, I believe my inquisitor has no idea what I'm talking about. I also wonder if my lack of knowledge about *The Death of a Salesman* has badly damaged my grade.

"So this is over," I say to myself as soon as I'm safely out of this dreaded examination room.

The last school days and our graduation ceremony pass quickly. Only one more thing is left: Party. We are permitted to use the art room for our celebration. Somebody brings a record player, and we dance to the latest tunes. Jitterbug is the craze, an import from America. Oh, how the skirts fly, as the girls twirl to the music! We are in an exuberant mood, especially those classmates who've had a few alcoholic drinks already. I have some sips, too, and since I'm not accustomed to drinking, the tiniest bit has its effect. It makes me feel as if my head is on a merry-go-round ride and my feet are not on steady ground. I seek a quieter place, away from my friends, where I can rest until the weird sensation leaves me. Helmut finds me in my corner by the staircase. He sits down next to me, and we have the most amiable conversation. Funny, when he doesn't want to impress a teacher, he can form the most intelligent, easy-to-understand sentences. Helmut and I get along famously. We are friends.

Actually, I'm on easy terms with all my male classmates. They know I have no romantic interest in them, and so they consider me a good, trustworthy pal.

For a while, I do have a boyfriend, a former classmate. But it's an on/off relationship. Several times, I get free of him, but the mothers meddle and push us back together. In the end, I decide dating is not worth the trouble. It infringes on my personal freedom.

*

Mama has a wonderful surprise, she says, and she's not going to tell what it is. We have to go to Rudow, on Saturday, after she comes home from work, and pick it up. I have absolutely no idea what "it" could be.

So, on Saturday afternoon, my mother and I take the trolley to Rudow, and then we walk … closer and closer to my old boyfriend's street. I hope she's not going to drag me to his house. But no, we stop before we get that far, and we go through someone else's open gate, and we meet a man who's puttering in his garden.

"*Guten Tag,*" says my mother. "We've come to pick up the bicycle."

"Oh, yes," he says, and he wipes his hands on his pants. "It's ready. Just wait here and I'll bring it out."

A bicycle? … Did Mama find out that the man wants to get rid of his bicycle? Is he selling it for cheap? … It would be nice for us to have something to ride around on. Yes, it would be nice.

I'm still deep in thought, when the man comes out of his shed, pushing a brand new, shiny, red bicycle toward us.

"Isn't it a beauty?" he asks.

"Yes," says my mother, taking hold of the handlebar and giving the bike an admiring look. "That's the one I ordered for my daughter."

"For me?" I ask. *No, it can't be. It must be a mistake.* "But Mama …"

"Yes, for you. Do you like it?"

"I love it. But … Why?"

She just stands there and smiles.

Finally I blurt out, "Thank you, thank you."

"Well, you may ride it home. I'll take the trolley, and then I'll pick up something from the butcher store on the way home. See you later."

I haven't been on a bike for years. I don't know if I still remember how to ride one. But after a few half-scary wiggles, I'm on my way. I feel like shouting,

"Look here, everyone! I have a bicycle. See how beautiful it is?" Though I pass lots of people, nobody pays attention to my new possession and me.

When I get home and show the bicycle to Gisela, she admires it. I detect no sign of jealousy. I don't think Gisela ever gets jealous.

Now that I have a set of wheels, I can join my friends on outings. Berlin has wonderful woods and lakes throughout the city. Those recreational places can be reached by public transportation, but it is so much more fun to ride there by bike. Especially, traveling in a group and talking and laughing and singing all the way. Get a bunch of Germans together, and they sing. It's in their blood.

Each excursion has to be planned. Who owns a telephone? Most of us don't. And since we don't see each other in class anymore, communication isn't so easy. Horst and I, with an idea in mind, get on our bikes and notify as many of our friends as possible. We have a lot of pedaling to do, to Britz, Rudow, and Buckow. Then, on the agreed upon day, at a certain hour in the morning, all who have time and are willing to participate meet at a convenient place, and then we're off to Grünau or to the Wannsee, Berlin's largest lake. During that summer of 1950, we enjoy freedom.

*

I've made up my mind to become an English teacher. My application has been mailed to the

Pädagogische Hochschule Berlin, the teacher's college. Soon after, I'm called in to write a brief essay about my intentions and why I've chosen English as my major, and what my other interests are. I mention painting and music. An interview follows. I'm nervous.

The gentleman who wants to chat with me, in his office, shows me an assortment of pictures. Some are watercolors; others are done in oil. There's also an ink drawing and something in pastels. I have to talk about the art forms and explain what I know about the techniques. That goes pretty well, in my opinion.

Then we discuss literature. Though I know the works and can easily talk about them, my mind goes blank when trying to remember a few of the authors' names.

Why doesn't he ask me something in English? I wonder. *I clearly stated in my application that I want to be an English teacher.*

My interviewer drones on about German literature.

I'm also good in French. If he doesn't want to hear my English, he can at least let me talk to him in French.

Finally, our conversation is over. I am excused. The good man gives me a warm smile, and I thank him. I cannot get out of the tiny interrogation chamber fast enough.

It doesn't take long until a letter comes in the mail with an explanation of why admission to the college has been postponed until the next semester. Actually, my two friends, who have asked for enrollment and been tested with me, receive the same answer. Preferential treatment, we are informed, has to be given to former servicemen, especially prisoners of war. They need to catch up first on their higher education.

Of course, I'm disappointed. I know I cannot hang around until my turn comes. Mama shouldn't have to support me longer than necessary.

After some deliberation, my mother and I decide I should study business instead. We choose a school in the Wilmersdorf district, which offers an accelerated program. Classes begin in September. And so, without regret, instead of teaching English, I enter the business world to deal with figures, my other favorite subject.

*

What are my goals? I want to advance in the corporation, GSW, which has built and now administers huge apartment complexes all over Berlin and in other parts of Germany. As employee of that company, I may have my name put on top of the list of apartment seekers. It sounds so very enticing. A nest of my own! After I've saved some money, of course.

"I'm not getting married until I'm at least thirty-two," I tell everybody. "I need time to concentrate on my career. I want to savor my independence."

Young men who vie for my attention get gently pushed away. If they agree to a platonic relationship, they are welcome. A love affair is out of the question.

Why then, only a few years later, do I let my supposedly hard-as-steel resolve be melted by a young American soldier, a corporal who plays the French horn in the 298th Army Band? I really can't tell.

We meet at the square dances, held in the service club, once a week. He loves to dance, and so do I. We both like the same kind of music. Conversation comes easy. We laugh a lot.

There's nothing pretentious about this young fellow who looks more like a kid than a soldier. He's not pushy; he behaves like a true gentleman. I don't have to fear sexual advances. Rather quickly, a comfortable feeling develops between us, and I start to consider him a good friend.

Somehow, out of the blue, after his brief furlough in Scotland to meet his mother's side of the family, he surprises me with a declaration of love and his desire to marry me.

You can't be serious! I think. *Have you been deaf? How often have you heard me say I don't want to get married for a long, long time?* Instead of chiding him, I ask for a chance to think it over. Actually, I'm hoping he'll forget the matter. But no, he's dead serious.

"You have to make up your mind fast. My time is almost up. They'll ship me back to the States unless I reenlist immediately. I would like to marry you in Berlin, in your own church."

My head is swimming. I have never thought of leaving Germany. And what about my plans? Should I really give up my freedom and yield to a man?

A few days later, I say, "Yes."

On June 26, 1954, my young corporal and I, in a white wedding coach, with Tante Uschi's and Onkel Martin's two little ones, Heidi and Helmut, riding along as flower children, make our way through the streets of Britz to the *Dorfkirche*, where I become Mrs. Thomas Priestley.

Four months later, very seasick, I'm crossing the Atlantic Ocean. I still cannot fully understand what has possessed me to the folly of getting married and wanting to make my home in New Jersey. Love is a strange condition. It messes up a person's brain, I assume.

Tom and I, both hard working and very thrifty, soon scrape together enough money for the down payment on a house, a small rancher on a whole acre of treeless meadow, in Mt. Laurel. Eventually, we are blessed with two lovely daughters, first Rosemarie, than Karen, and I have no regrets that I've gotten married ten years sooner than originally planned.

A few days before my 49th wedding anniversary, I find myself in a new position. I am, rather unexpectedly, a widow.

After the funeral guests have departed, and I've done my share of crying and screaming at the evil spirits that must be hovering somewhere above, I declare, "Get hold of yourself, Eva! Life goes on. You have a class to teach tomorrow – and don't forget choir practice."

Thus summoning my old can-do attitude, I decide to redesign life to my own liking and to face the future with confidence.

Eva, the girl, has learned to be tough. Eva, the woman, is tougher.

ACKNOWLEDGEMENTS

My special thanks go to my sister, Gisela, for helping me put certain events into chronological order.

I would also like to take the opportunity to praise those high school friends who made a sincere effort to remember the sequence and approximate times of school-related happenings. Strangely, we all came up with different clues.

Many thanks go to Tom Hepler, my faithful student, who more than once came to the rescue when I had computer problems, and to my good friend, Alison Gregory, who read the first draft of my manuscript with care and pointed out errors.

The students of my Wednesday and Thursday creative writing classes at the Mt. Laurel Senior Center should not be forgotten. They were the ones who, patiently, for an entire year and more, listened to the story of my life.

And how could I possibly leave out Christina Wood, my talented granddaughter, who came to my rescue after all the writing was done? Yes, Christina, I thank you for helping me design the book cover and with final details.

Made in the USA
Middletown, DE
08 July 2015